The Man Who Lived with a Giant

THE **MAN** WHO LIVED WITH A **GIANT**
STORIES FROM JOHNNY NEYELLE, DENE ELDER

ALANA FLETCHER & MORRIS NEYELLE, *EDITORS*

P Polynya Press   An imprint of University of Alberta Press

Published by

The University of Alberta Press
Ring House 2
Edmonton, Alberta, Canada   T6G 2E1
www.uap.ualberta.ca

Copyright © 2019 The University of
Alberta Press

LIBRARY AND ARCHIVES CANADA
CATALOGUING IN PUBLICATION

Title: The man who lived with a giant :
     stories from Johnny Neyelle, Dene elder /
     Alana Fletcher and Morris Neyelle,
     editors.
Names: Fletcher, Alana, 1987- editor. |
     Neyelle, Morris, 1951- editor.
Identifiers: Canadiana (print) 20190057637 |
     Canadiana (ebook) 20190057718 |
     ISBN 9781772124088 (softcover) |
     ISBN 9781772124668 (EPUB) |
     ISBN 9781772124675 (Kindle) |
     ISBN 9781772124682 (PDF)
Subjects: LCSH: Chipewyan Indians—
     Northwest Territories—Folklore. |
     LCSH: Chipewyan Indians—Northwest
     Territories—History. | LCSH: Oral
     tradition—Northwest Territories.
Classification: LCC E99.C59 M36 2019 |
     DDC 398.2089/972—dc23

First edition, first printing, 2019.
First printed and bound in Canada by
Houghton Boston Printers, Saskatoon,
Saskatchewan.
Copyediting and proofreading by
Kirsten Craven.

University of Alberta Press is committed
to protecting our natural environment.
As part of our efforts, this book is printed
on Enviro Paper: it contains 100% post-
consumer recycled fibres and is acid- and
chlorine-free.

University of Alberta Press gratefully
acknowledges the support received for its
publishing program from the Government
of Canada, the Canada Council for the Arts,
and the Government of Alberta through the
Alberta Media Fund.

Canada   Canada Council   Conseil des Arts
          for the Arts   du Canada

Alberta
Government

Contents

II Oral Histories from the Life of Johnny Neyelle

Preface

THIS BOOK, like any oral history collection, is the product of many important relationships: the relationship of the stories to all Sahtu Dene people, past and present; that of the storyteller and his son; the relationship of the two editors; and those among the editors and the support network that helped make this book a reality.

This book has been a long-time project, and its arrival has been eagerly anticipated by the Neyelle family and their whole community. It was in the 1980s that Morris first began recording Johnny's stories on cassette tapes with the goal of one day writing a book to share with his people. After his father's death, Morris began the laborious process of transcribing and translating the recordings. When Alana, at that time a doctoral candidate studying the relationship between environmentalism and oral history, came to stay with Morris's family for fieldwork in Déline in 2014, Morris asked her to help him turn what he had done into a published book. Alana returned to Déline to stay with Morris in the summer of 2015, when he shared with her the transcriptions, family photos, and scans of Johnny's diary that he had collected.

Since that time, numerous phone calls, Facebook chats, emails, and ground packages have been exchanged between us as we built the collection that would become *The Man Who Lived with a Giant: Stories from Johnny Neyelle, Dene Elder*. The close relationship we were able to establish does not usually grow out of academic research by one party in the community of the other. Both of us are so grateful to each other for the trust, openness, and generosity shown on the one side and the transparency, humbleness, and responsibility maintained on the other. We very much appreciate each other's hard work in taking on this opportunity to carry on Dene traditions in a good way.

We are very grateful to our families and our loved ones for their willingness to support and inform this project. All of our love and gratitude goes out to you, and you know who you are. We also want to say a big *máhci cho* to Danny Gaudet, Deb Simmons, Miggs Morris, and Lynda Lange for supporting our Northwest Territories Arts Council application. *Máhci* to the Arts Council for the funding it provided, and thank you to Peter Midgley, our anonymous readers, and the whole team at University of Alberta Press for knowing a good book when they saw it and pushing to make it the best it could be.

Johnny Neyelle and his storytelling deserve our greatest acknowledgements for inspiring this important book. Had he not developed his stories so masterfully and shared them so generously, this book would not be here today. We are also obligated to all the Dene people: to the ancestors who passed these stories on to us, and to the future generations to whom we pass them on. To all the communities of the Sahtu (Déline, Tulita, K'áhbamñtúé, Rádeyîlîkóé, and Tåegōhtî), to all the people mentioned in these stories, and to Dene readers everywhere, *máhci cho* for letting us share and promote the Dene culture.

We hope this book will bring new understanding to many people in and beyond the Sahtu. Maybe it will be adopted in elementary and high school curricula in the Sahtu, in which capacity it could be readily available to young people, the most important audience for its stories. The stories in this collection offer much to non-Dene readers, as well, though it may not be readily apparent. As Johnny says, no matter who you are, where you are from, or what you think you need to know, "if you grab hold of a story and put it in your heart, you will benefit from it in the future."

FROM THE OUTSET, we wanted Johnny Neyelle's words to remain
the focus of this book, and the book's structure reflects this. We have
provided a short overview of the Sahtu Dene for readers who are not
familiar with the peoples of the Northwest Territories. Following that,
Morris briefly introduces his father and the reasons why a book like
this is necessary. Then it is Johnny's turn to tell us a little about Dene
philosophy and storytelling. These elements will provide readers with
a sound framework with which to read Johnny's stories.

For those who are interested in exploring the scholarly underpin-
nings of the work, Alana has provided an afterword in which she talks
about the methodology behind editing the stories. This is followed by
a useful genealogy of the extended Neyelle family, and by a glossary of
North Slavey words that appear in the text.

The Sahtu Dene

The Sahtúot'ine, Sahtu Dene, or Bear Lake people are a traditionally
nomadic group who historically moved throughout their territory
following the resources available in different seasons. This territory

occupies a large part of what is now Canada's Northwest Territories, bordered by and blending with the lands of the K'áshogot'ine (Hare) and Shúhtaot'ine (Mountain) Dene peoples. According to oral accounts, the Dene have occupied this area since time immemorial, and archaeological accounts show evidence of Dene habitation as far back as two to three thousand years ago.

The Sahtu are one of the Northern Athapaskan language groups, speaking a dialect called North Slavey. They have linguistic, spiritual, and political affinities with other Dene peoples, most immediately with other Northern Athapaskan speaking groups (Chipewyan, Tłicho, Yellowknives, and Dehcho Dene) but also with Pacific Coast and Southern Athapaskan speakers in the continental United States (the Diné and Indé, among others).

Johnny Neyelle, a respected Elder from the Sahtu Dene community of Déline, was known throughout the Sahtu and beyond as a gifted hunter, craftsman, and musician, but especially as a storyteller. These are his versions of some of the stories from his culture that pass on everything from hunting and trapping techniques to political and ethical frameworks to spiritual cosmologies through the generations.

Telling My Dad's Story MORRIS NEYELLE

First of all, this book has to do with my dad, how way back around 1970 or 1980 he started to tell me all his stories. I told him that I would write about it. Then I realized that storytelling was changing and that kids weren't coming to listen to the Elders' stories anymore; they want to learn more technical stuff. So that's a big reason why I put it in a book, so that my kids and other kids can learn from it.

It's not about what I can make from the book in terms of money. It's how I can teach Dene people about our life in the past. That's one of my life goals. In the past, Dene storytellers would tell their stories over and over until the people had every word memorized. But everything's changing now, so, before we lose the stories, I want people to write about it, paint it, record it, anything to bring that forward in the modern world. My way of talking is to always encourage my people to write our stories, to carry the traditional way of life into the future with us.

When I gave my dad my cassette tapes back in the '80s, I just told him, record whatever needs to be recorded. The stories in this book are the ones my dad thought were most important. I still have a bunch of diaries from my dad with more stories and more teachings in them. But, for me, one of the most important stories is about his dream from the 1940s. He said he had never told anybody that one before he told me. The things he had seen and what he witnessed when he was really sick are, I think, telling us something about the next life, so it's really important. And most of my dad's dreams came true!

My goal is for the younger people to read this book, because a lot of them don't know how we actually lived or how our ancestors lived in the past. And it's up to them to educate themselves through this book we are writing for them.

Story and Dene Philosophy   JOHNNY NEYELLE

What I will be talking to you about are the stories of Elders of the past, how they lived, and how they passed on their knowledge so Dene people could survive. I want you to listen well to what I am saying. The Elders of the past always talked the truth that comes straight from the heart. Whatever Elders are talking about, the younger people should always try to understand it and then live it, so they can go into the future and not forget who they are.

The Elders always knew a lot of things. From just the way you talked, the way you worked, they would know about your life. Sometimes when you talked—if you didn't watch what you were saying—the Elders didn't like it. They don't want you to talk like that. So they would teach you and correct the mistakes you made. That's what my dad, Jacque Neyelle, told me. When you talk, talk the truth. Don't make yourself too proud of what you did. Be humble.

The time will come when you will remember what I said in the future. Maybe in the future, younger people might learn from what I'm saying and use it. I'm not saying I was the only one that Elders talked to; a lot of people listened to them in the past. They knew that if you grab hold of a story and put it in your heart, you will benefit from it in the future. Our fathers, our great ancestors kept all the stories in their hearts. Even though they never wrote them down, still they remembered them. That's how they passed on the stories for thousands of years.

Itá used to tell us that man is made to work outside, to hunt, trap, fish, and learn how to survive the wilderness. That's what we as men are made for. Women are there to take care of the kids and the house, to clean, cook, and keep the fire burning inside. After every lecture given to us by my dad, he would light his pipe. Then it was my *éne* who would talk to us.

"My sons," she would start. Then she would tell us how, in the past, people would have dreams in which they would be given *įk'ǫ*, great powers, that they would depend on for their survival out on the land. "But, my sons," she would say, "if you are not gifted like that, the stories that your *betá* is giving to you are like a good road he has made for you to follow. It's a long road with no end. That's the kind of road he has built. To walk on this road does not mean everything will work out for you. There will be problems, disasters, heartaches, and pains to go through, but, God willing, you will make it to the very end where you will see your grey hair. That's what your dad is talking about."

The stories I'm telling you are not stories from today. They were passed on from generation to generation. And I want you to give this story to your kids, too, and so on and so on for many more generations. Your grandfather, my dad, told these stories to me, and the time has come for me to tell you. That's why I always ask you to come visit me. My dad asked me to give these stories to my kids when they were grown up. I want you to learn the stories well so you can pass them on to your kids.

I'm not going to tell the same story day after day, so learn and listen well, because I'm going to say each one once. That's how it was in the past. It's like the Creator's speech that the Elders would teach us—a lot of Elders told me that, and it's very true, very true. Stories like the ones I tell you are good for the younger people. Whoever knows stories like these should tell them to the young people.

Really, it's all about living: how to live together as man and wife, how to live in a foreign place, how to stay alive by trapping and hunting. All of that my dad taught us. A lot of times I went travelling with him in the cold winter nights. All the time he was teaching me then, which I only realized later. I am thankful for that. *Máhci.* Now today, I'm thinking I did really well in my life. I didn't really experience too difficult of a hardship in my life. Whatever happens in life happens, and I'm thankful about what's happened to me. That's why I'm saying this.

All these kinds of stories I'm telling, if you listen to them and follow their guide, they and the Creator will help you through your life.

I Sacred and Traditional Stories

THERE ONCE WAS A TRIBE OF PEOPLE living in the mountains. They would hunt and fish and move around wherever there was plenty of hunting and fishing for their survival. This was in the time of the dinosaurs, so the mountain people always had to be prepared for the unexpected.

One day in the summer, two brothers went out hunting. They went out into areas where they knew there was usually plenty of wild game. While they were hunting, they saw a giant man coming toward them. They got very scared and ran into a cave to hide from the giant man, thinking they might get eaten alive. In the cave, the giant couldn't get them because the cave opening was too small.

The giant said, "*Betsée*, come back out here. I'm not going to hurt you." Even though they were very scared, the older brother came back out to the giant, leaving his scared younger brother behind inside the cave. The older brother begged and begged his younger brother to come out, but he wouldn't. So the giant pooped against the cave entrance, trapping the younger brother inside it forever.

With that done, the giant took the older brother with him and continued on his travels. The giant was very kind to the older brother and always fed him and took care of him. They travelled the land and the giant taught him well too!

One summer day as the giant and the older brother were walking among the bushes in the mountains, the giant said, "*Betsée*, there are two rabbits walking close by—be quiet and I'll see if I can get them." The giant grabbed his bow and arrow and stalked the rabbits. After a while, he took two quick shots and got both of them. The giant said to the older brother, "*Betsée*, we'll make fire here."

They made fire and cooked the two animals, which the giant kept calling rabbits. The older brother was confused because he knew they weren't rabbits—they were cow moose, which to the giant looked as small as rabbits do to normal-sized people! When the cow moose were cooked, the giant grabbed one and stripped it and swallowed it whole, just like it was a rabbit. Then the giant grabbed the other moose, which was a little smaller because it was a calf. He presented it to the older brother, but, because he was so small, he couldn't eat all of the meat that was given to him and only ate a small piece. The giant looked at his new-found friend with exasperation and said, "*Betsée*, why are you living in a world of small things only?"

The giant and the older brother continued to travel the world together, hunting and fishing. Wherever there was food, that's where they went. As years and years went by, they taught and shared everything. One day, while they were travelling, they came to a large lake where they saw another giant checking net, with his wife and child in a teepee back on the mainland. The giant warned the older brother, saying, "*Betsée*, when we giants see each other, we have to fight to the death."

"*Betsée*," he continued, "I need your help. I want you to cover me with snow. Then you go see if you can make the giant angry. He will chase you toward me, and then I can kill him."

The older brother covered his giant friend with snow and then he went to meet the other giant, who was still checking net. When he got close, he turned himself into a fox and, in that form, he started bugging the giant by stealing his fish. He kept at it until the giant got really angry.

Yelling, "What is it that's bugging me!" the giant grabbed his scooper and started chasing the fox-shaped older brother. The fox ran toward his giant friend who was hiding under the snow. The ice thundered and cracked behind him from the heavy footsteps of the giant running. When the fox jumped over his giant friend, the giant chasing him jumped too—and that's when the hiding giant burst out of the snow and attacked his giant enemy! They fought and fought until a time came when it looked like the older brother's giant friend was beginning to lose.

The giant yelled to his human friend, "*Betsée*, I think I will be beaten! Can you help me by cutting his ankle sinew with your beaver-tooth knife?" Immediately the older brother grabbed his beaver-tooth knife and sliced the ankles of the giant who was killing his friend. The enemy giant fell to his knees. The friendly giant got up, grabbed his giant enemy, and stabbed him in the heart. And that's where he died—that enemy giant was finally killed.

Even though the giant friend was injured badly, he and the older brother went back to the teepee of the dead giant, where they met the giant's wife and son. The giant attacked the wife and killed her too. Then the giant told his friend to kill the dead giant's son, but he was too small, so the giant did it.

The giant and the older brother continued to roam the country together. The giant would often put his human friend on his shoulders or on his head, so he could hunt the giant louse that was on the giant's head. To the older brother, the louse was as big as a *tehk'áe*, a muskrat, so he could easily find and kill it. One night, as they were sleeping out in the wilderness, the giant friend said, "*Betsée*, I'm badly injured by the other giant and it looks like I'm not going to survive much longer. I want you to go look for whatever family you have left."

The older brother looked at his giant friend lying in front of the open fire, and he got really sad because he couldn't help his injured friend. The giant instructed the brother, saying, "Here, take this arrow of mine. Every time you spend a night, stake it on the ground. Whichever way it falls in the morning, that's the direction you should go. This will bring you back to your parents."

Then the giant gave his friend some bone grease and told him, "*Betsée*, eat this bone grease whenever you're hungry—but always leave a little piece for tomorrow, don't eat it all. When morning comes around, the piece will always be the same size as before you ate from it. As long as you don't eat it all, it should last a lifetime. And even if you're really hungry, do not eat any berries."

He also gave his friend a birchbark bowl, telling him, "Whenever there's a war, cover yourself and your family with this bowl. It should protect you from your enemies." With that, the giant gave his friend one last piece of information. "Watch the sunset as you are travelling," he said. "When you see it turn a reddish colour all around the universe, you will know that I have died."

The older brother really didn't want to leave his giant friend behind, but he knew it was time to go. He packed the few things he had, along with the gifts his giant friend had given him, and he left. He was wondering about the instructions that came with the gifts. The first night he spent alone, he staked the arrow in the ground and went to sleep by the open fire. When morning came, he noticed the arrow had fallen. The way it was pointing was the direction he started walking.

He kept walking and walking, spending nights here and there. Every night he staked the arrow in the ground and whichever way the arrow fell he would go in that direction in the morning. He went on like this for days, weeks, months.

One day, he was tired of the bone grease he was eating all the time, and he decided to eat some berries. He remembered that his giant friend had told him not to eat any berries, and he wondered what would happen. As soon as he ate the berries, he could feel the ground shaking. All of a sudden a pack of huge wolves, dogs, bears, and other animals were upon him, attacking him. As fast as he could, he climbed a tree to get away. He cried out to his giant friend in fear, "*Betsée*, giant wolves and dogs are attacking me! Do something before they chew the tree down and kill me!"

From far away, the giant heard his human friend calling his name. He called to the animals, asking them to come to him and leave the young man alone. The giant wolves, dogs, bears, squirrels, and other animals suddenly stopped attacking the older brother. They stood silently for a moment and then started turning away. The young man thought, "No wonder he asked me not to eat the berries!" He climbed back down from the giant tree and started walking on his way again.

The older brother spent many more days travelling, going in the direction the arrow fell, until one day he finally found his people again. But his people were very scared of him when they first met because a long time had passed since he got lost and they couldn't remember him. He told them what had happened: how he and his younger brother hid from the giant in a cave, how his younger brother was trapped, and how he was taken by the giant. He began to settle back in to life with his people.

Even after coming home, the older brother remembered the instructions of the giant. He would always save a piece of his bone grease, making sure he didn't eat it all. The next morning it would always be the same, back to its original size again. Through the hard years when there was no food, this bone grease pulled the people through. One day, though, a hungry child found the bone grease. He was so hungry he ate it all, leaving none behind. The child died, and the bone grease was lost forever.

There were wars between different tribal people all the time. When wars started, the older brother would get his people together and cover them with the birchbark bowl his giant friend had given him. It would protect them from the enemy's sight, and they would all be safe. The older brother used the gifts given to him by his giant friend whenever they were needed, especially during wars and starvation periods. He travelled with his people for years, hunting and fishing.

One evening when he was outside, he noticed the colours changing in the sky. All around the universe, the sky was turning reddish. He knew then that his giant friend had died. He sat down and wept bitterly, knowing he would never see his giant friend again.

This is one of the Dene stories from the time of the dinosaurs, when the world was new.

Bone Grease from the Sky

How the Animals Became Fat

PEOPLE AND ANIMALS BEGAN TO STARVE when ice started forming on the land. People didn't know what to do. Two of these people were brothers who were roaming the land, sleeping wherever they were when night fell on them.

The younger brother said to the older brother, "Brother, I am so hungry. I need something to eat!" The older brother, pitying him, said, "Well then, I will talk to the stars that are in the sky, and see what I can do."

As the younger brother was getting ready to sleep, his older brother walked away a little ways. He started yelling as loud as he could, talking to the stars and especially to Yíhda, the Big Dipper. He said, "Yíhda, you told me if I ever needed anything I could call on you—and I'm calling now." When he came back, he told his younger brother, "I have talked to Yíhda. Now we will see what happens."

Soon the two brothers heard a loud windy sound from the sky, the sound of something falling. They saw a huge gigantic ball falling and wondered what it was. It landed close to them and rolled past them down the hill. The older brother had a club. As the ball rolled by, he hit the side of it and a chunk of grease came away from it. The brothers ate it and found that it was the finest bone grease they had ever tasted. The giant ball of grease continued to roll on into the lake, and the brothers fell asleep.

The next day, they saw a huge piece of bone grease floating in the centre of a medium-sized pond off the lake. The brothers knew all the animals were starving too, and they wanted to share the gift of grease. They made a big bonfire around the pond and heated up all the rocks around its edge. Then they rolled the hot rocks into the pond, melting the grease slowly. They did this for days upon days, until all the bone grease melted and they could see grease floating on top of the water. Then the older brother summoned all the animals, saying, "Come, all of you who are hungry, feast with us and have some bone grease!"

There was a little channel connecting the pond to another pond, and the older brother told his younger brother to sit on the other side and keep watch as the animals began to swim toward the bone grease. Soon all the animals on Earth begin to show up. They started swimming across the channel into the bone grease pond and feeding on the bone grease.

Soon a porcupine and a beaver showed up. The porcupine said, "My beaver friend, can you help me swim across?" The beaver said, "Okay, sit on my back and I will swim across with you." The beaver swam across with the porcupine on top of him and the porcupine rested there while they were both eating. When they got back across the channel the porcupine said, "Where our bodies touched there will be no fat." That's why, to this day, the beaver only gets fat in the front area and none on his back, and the porcupine only gets fat on his back area and none on his front—because that's where their bodies touched when they swam across.

More and more animals started showing up and swimming to the bone grease and feeding. When the rabbit showed up, he swam across to the bone grease and started feeding and feeding. When he got back across the channel, he could barely walk because he was so filled up with grease. He started to cry and moan in pain as he sat there on the ground. The younger brother grabbed the rabbit and rinsed the grease from his fur, saying, "You're here to feed yourself, not cry about it!" That's why today when a rabbit is fat only a couple streaks of fat show on its neck and most of the fat is in its stomach.

Some of the animals got there early and ate the fat while it was still warm. Today, those animals have fat that does not freeze too much in the winter. Other animals that showed up very late, when the grease was starting to freeze again, today have fat that freezes fast.

It was when the grease in the pond started to freeze that the bull caribou showed up. He swam to the bone grease and started feeding, but he had to work hard to break up the slab of freezing fat. That's why, to this day, the caribou's fat freezes fast. It's the same for the big horn sheep. The reason they showed up so late to the bone grease feast was because their land was the farthest away.

So all the animals eventually swam across and fed themselves from the bone grease from the sky. This all happened by a lake called Tugǫ́túé, or Keller Lake. When you set net in that lake, the ice comes out in chunks as you chisel, just the same way the bone grease chunk came out of the giant ball that fell from the sky.

This is one of the legends of the Sahtúot'ine.

Doo-roo-tseh, the Medicine Man

THERE WAS ONCE AN ANCESTOR OF OURS who was a very
powerful medicine man. He was a kind of leader for the Shúhtaot'ine,
the mountain people. His name was Doo-roo-tseh.

Doo-roo-tseh would tell people when we should move to different
places—that's the way it went. We were moving from place to place
in the mountains, where there was big game and lakes with lots of fish
in them.

Once, as we were travelling all around, we sensed we were not the
only ones in the area. We sensed that there might be some other tribes
following us and spying on us. Doo-roo-tseh's sons were ahead of us
with an Elder. They hunted, and we would camp whenever they got big
game. We were travelling with our dog packs, following a little behind
Doo-roo-tseh's sons, when it got dark and they decided to overnight.

That night they camped by a place they had gotten a sheep. They
had an open-pit fire burning with spruce boughs all around it, with
fresh meat cooking on the open fire. All of a sudden they saw a fox
coming out of the darkness with a bright light streaking from its tail.
The fox ran all around their camp and the light encircled it. Then

the fox disappeared. The circle looked like one of the northern lights wrapped right around them. That's when they knew there were Nahʔane nearby, Yukon people who were kidnappers.

Even though Doo-roo-tseh was all the way back at the camp, he knew the situation his sons were in. He kind of patted the Nahʔane powers down with his powers, so the Nahʔane had to back off from attacking his sons. But ahead of them his sons, the good hunters, were very afraid and yelled at each other. "That fire is all around us," they said. "It's the powers of the Nahʔane! We need to do something if we want to get out of this alive!" They looked at the Elder who was with them and yelled at him, saying, "You always talk about the fox— why don't you do something about this fire that the fox spread all around us?"

The Elder stood silent for a moment. Then he said, "Grab your packs and let's go. I'll see what I can do." They walked out to the fire line the fox had made. When they got there, the Elder took off his fur hat and took a swipe at the fire. The fire then recoiled with a sizzling sound and vanished. The two sons and the Elder were draped in the darkness of the night. They stayed together like that, near the ridge, and stayed awake until daylight came.

When daylight arrived, they started heading back to the main camp. Then they noticed a fox following them a little off side from them. They knew it was the Nahʔane kidnappers again, using their medicine powers to spy on them. When they got back to camp, they told Doo-roo-tseh what had happened. Doo-roo-tseh was mad that the Nahʔane were still trying to make trouble despite his powers. He said, "We can't just sit here and do nothing. We have to do something about them—we have to protect ourselves."

Then Doo-roo-tseh started preparing himself for the long medicine battle he was about to face. He wondered to himself, "Why did my sons fear the kidnappers so much?" He said, "I will see that for myself." Then he invited his sons and the Elders out to the open fire. Doo-roo-tseh said to them, "I will never let the Shúhtaot'ine give themselves up to the kidnappers." Then he started chanting and singing.

Doo-roo-tseh warned the people, "Don't try to use your powers to help me, because one of the Nahʔane has very powerful eyesight that could take your life." As he was singing, one of the tribal warriors fell face down, unconscious. Doo-roo-tseh yelled, "Didn't I just tell you not to look? Now I have to get back your eyesight from the Nahʔane!" He said, "I'll try to get it back, but the Nahʔane kidnapper has an otter pelt with a long tail that he's using to knock away whatever we throw at him."

Doo-roo-tseh thought for a moment and then asked one of his sons to give him gunpowder, lots of it. With his spiritual powers, he sent the gunpowder toward the Nahʔane. As the kidnapper was swinging his otter pelt at the gunpowder flares to push them away, Doo-roo-tseh grabbed the eyesight of the fallen warrior from inside the Nahʔane's otter-tail pelt. He sent the eyesight back to the warrior, who came to right away. Doo-roo-tseh told him, "Don't ever disobey me again." Then he continued on chanting.

Doo-roo-tseh thought he would try to read the Nahʔane's thoughts and discover why they were there. So he tied three small poles together and placed an eagle feather on top. He raised the three poles around the outside of the burning fire, and asked his people not to go near it. He kept chanting and singing, rolling up his shirt sleeves as he jumped over the fire and grabbed the base of the three poles, just below the eagle feather.

The people couldn't really see what he was doing, but they saw blood streaming down Doo-roo-tseh's wrist. Doo-roo-tseh said, "That's the bad thoughts the Nahʔane have." Doo-roo-tseh was tearing up the bad thoughts and making them weak. Along with the blood, the people could hear sounds and see lights of many colours coming up from his wrist. "Their thoughts are getting weaker," said Doo-roo-tseh.

Then he asked, "Does anyone have a white stone called *bega*? I can use it to send the Nahʔane back where they came from." One of the

Elders had a *bega*, a white stone, and gave it to Doo-roo-tseh. Doo-roo-tseh sent the stone toward the Nahʔane, saying, "It will grab all their thoughts and bring them back toward their land." After he did this he said, "If you don't hear anything from them, the Nahʔane, in the next two days, it means that it worked—they left for their land." "They will also leave some sort of markings showing they have left," he continued, "so be on a lookout for that."

Over the next few days everything quieted down, and people started hunting again without any fear. Finally, on one hunt, they came upon an old campsite of the Nahʔane. They saw sticks with moss on the end sticking out of the ground, rows and rows of them, pointing in the direction the Nahʔane were heading. "It looks like they went home," Doo-roo-tseh said.

So that ended the battle that would have happened if it weren't for Doo-roo-tseh's medicine powers, which sent the Nahʔane home without any bloodshed.

Kidnapped Woman Escapes

LONG AGO, before the arrival of the Europeans, there was a tribe
of people who were descendants of the Shúhtaot'ine, the mountain
people who roamed the Mackenzie Mountains. There was a fish lake
called Tɬok'á náʔa, which means grass standing up, and another lake
called Taʔąle where a lot of people gathered to harvest fish.

At one time, some of the mountain people decided to go into the
mountains to hunt for bigger game like sheep, caribou, and moose.
They had to hunt enough to put up food for the coming winter, since
winters were always severe—a lot of people could starve during the
winter. One of the elderly women had two nieces who went into
the mountains with her. They went into the mountain range called
Begáyué. At the end of the range there's a place called *k'áté* or Willow
Flats. That's where the old woman and her nieces settled to make
drymeat with whatever they could hunt.

Back then, the Shúhtaot'ine were in an ongoing war with the
Nahʔane, the Yukon people, so they had to be very cautious and alert
at all times. They had a chief hunter, the *bedzikat'į*, who did all the
hunting for them and who would always lead them into good hunting

Johnny Neyelle's cabin near k'áté, Willow Flats.

Johnny Neyelle's tent at the spring hunting grounds near k'áté, Willow Flats, circa 1987.

Johnny Neyelle holds up a muskrat at the spring hunting grounds near k'áté, *circa 1987.*

territory. He would tell the people whether to set snares for moose, caribou, or bears, and whatever the people caught they would use for food, clothing, and tools. Nothing was ever wasted.

One day, the *bedzikat'į* was leading his people ahead on a hunt. Some other hunters walked with him and the women and children followed behind. Suddenly, some Nahʔane who had been stalking them burst out of the bushes and started attacking the people from behind, killing everybody they could see. *Bedzikat'į*, the chief hunter, heard his people's screams and turned to see the Nahʔane's attack.

He was too late to help his slain people, so he started running away as fast as he could. His snowshoes were heavy, and the Nahʔane warriors began to catch up to him. *Bedzikat'į* saw a river close by and thought, "If I could just make it to the river, I can survive the attack!" He ran toward the river, but he tripped over his feet and fell down.

The Nahʔane were almost upon him. He got up just in time and plunged into the river, where he used his medicine powers to travel swiftly down the river like a fish. The Nahʔane warriors also had powers and used them to try to fish the *bedzikat'į* out of the river, but the *bedzikat'į* had a little more medicine power than any of the Nahʔane, so he was always one step ahead of them.

Finally, the *bedzikat'į* got to the main camp where all his people, the Shúhtaot'ine were. He called out to them, saying, "The Yukon people who always play with us are playing with us now—and I'm the only survivor left!" And, with that, he kept on travelling down the river like a fish.

The two girls who were with their aunt started panicking. Their aunt threw both of them inside the caribou-hide teepee, and then she started chopping down willows with a tool like a stick with a hook at the end of it. She got herself a good piece of wooden club to fight with. Suddenly, she heard screams. She turned and saw her people the Shúhtaot'ine being slaughtered by the Nahʔane, dying like flies. She yelled to her nieces, "Stay inside! Don't go out!" and she started fighting the Nahʔane. They were attacking her from both sides.

With her back to the teepee she was protecting, she was encircled all about by stunted willows. She noticed their sharp, frozen points. She grabbed the frozen barbs and used them to snag the ends of the Nahʔane's snowshoes and pull them toward her until they fell down in the deep snow, when she would club them to death. She was killing all who came toward her, but more and more kept coming. She cried out, "I'm only protecting my two nieces!" but they kept coming—so she kept on killing them. Finally, an Elder of the Nahʔane yelled out to them, saying, "Leave them alone." Then the warriors stopped attacking.

The two girls and their aunt looked around them and realized they were the only survivors of the whole Shúhtaot'ine camp. The Nahʔane took the three women back to their territory, where the two girls were married to two of the warriors. Back then, if you were a man who wanted to live with a woman, you would put a necklace around her neck—that declared that you were her owner. And that's what the two Nah?ane warriors did with the two nieces.

By now, the *bedzikat'į*, the one who escaped on the river, had made it to the main Shúhtaot'ine settlement along the Dehcho, the Mackenzie River. He told them the story of the killings, and how the three women had become part of the Nah?ane tribe. When the Shúhtaot'ine heard the news about the battle, they became very angry and wanted revenge. One of the Shúhtaot'ine medicine men decided to bring about that revenge. One evening, when he was singing and chanting some songs to the beat of his drum, he told his people, "I have sent ice and cooked rawhide to the Nah?ane. They won't feel the revenge curse it brings this year, but they will surely feel it next year."

That first year went well for the Nah?ane people and the three women they had kidnapped. They travelled together all over the treeline close to the mountains, staying over wherever they snared or killed big game. The aunt and her nieces dried moose meat, tanned hides for clothing, made tools, and cached most of the dried meat for the winter, knowing as they did how winters could be harsh. But, during the second winter, things started changing for the Nah?ane. Even though they had fresh meat, they started eating cooked rawhide. This was the curse the Shúhtaot'ine medicine man had set beginning to emerge.

Winter came and it started getting colder and colder. The Nah?ane were beginning to starve even though they had food. The rawhide curse was a starving curse, and the ice curse was a freezing curse—and the Nah?ane were beginning to feel the effects of both. At the end of the treeline, probably at Begáhdé or a little further up, at *weh-zia*, *ni-cha*, or one of the big rivers that comes out from Náts'uhch'o, that's where all of this was happening. The Nah?ane were camping in that area while everything was getting worse and worse.

As it got colder, they started preparing to go overland to a place called *tse-tsee* flats, where there was a food cache stored. On the way overland, the curse hit them full force. It got colder and colder, and everything in sight froze solid. But the men still tried to keep moving, breaking a trail with their snowshoes while the women pulled the moose-skin sleds of belongings and children behind.

That's when the oldest of the two kidnapped sisters realized what was happening—she recognized the Shúhtaot'ine medicine man's curse. She told her youngest sister that she wanted to go home. "I want to try to escape these Nahʔane people!" she said. The younger sister said to her older sister, "I can't come with you. I have two small kids and I can't leave them behind." The older sister thought hard about it and then she decided to escape on her own. She told her sister and her aunt, "I will be making fire every once in a while. When I'm ahead of you overland, you will know I'm around when you see a fire burning. When you no longer see fires burning, you'll know I have escaped and gone back to my people, the Shúhtaot'ine." And, with that, she went on ahead.

As the younger niece and her aunt were travelling overland, all through the coldest time of the year, they would stop wherever they saw a fire. They knew their sister was still going ahead of them, making fire. They kept on going, coming across her burning fires, until they stopped finding fire. Her aunt looked far into the distance, but she could see no more fire burning ahead. Then she knew her niece had made the turn for her escape. She decided then and there she would follow her niece and try to escape too. She turned and started trying to find her niece.

Meanwhile, the oldest sister was trying to find the old trail back to her people. When she finally found it, she travelled all night and all day. Then she reached a place where the Shúhtaot'ine had camped in the fall—she remembered it by a pile of moose hair that was still there. She crept into the old campsite and lay down to sleep.

She slept almost all night before she heard a noise like a raven calling and opened a sleepy eye to see what was there. To her surprise, it was her aunt walking by, crying! She jumped up and called out to her aunt, saying, "Everything will be okay! Don't cry." She made fire for them to warm up to, but her aunt kept on crying. Eventually, her aunt calmed down. She told her niece, "When the sun came up and shone so

colourfully on the mountains, I could see the place where so many of
our people were killed years ago because of the war. That was why I
was crying."

The older sister started scavenging for food, gathering whatever
roots and plants she could find and boiling them to drink the broth.
They did whatever it took to survive while they travelled the old trail
along the river. Day and night they travelled, making fire along the
way to warm up. There were no traces of animals they could snare—no
rabbit, no porcupine, no gophers. The only animals around at all were
squirrels. So, wherever there were squirrel tracks, that's where they
would overnight.

It was getting tougher and tougher for them to get food when
finally one evening the aunt couldn't walk anymore. She was just too
weak. They stopped and camped for a while and the older sister tried
very hard to get more food, mostly snaring squirrels. They stayed there
for several weeks until her aunt got her strength back, and, finally, one
day she tried walking again. "I think I can travel again now," she told
her niece. So they started travelling again. It was also getting warmer
now, and they knew the spring weather was near.

There is a river called *weh-zia* just past Wrigley, and that's where the
aunt and her niece had stopped to regain strength. When they started
walking again, the aunt recognized some of the land in the area. She
said, "Just over the ridge there is a fish lake where sometimes our people
used to harvest fish." They started overland to check it out. Once they
got to the top of the ridge overlooking the fish lake, they rested again.
The aunt fell asleep right away, since it was a warm and tiring trek.

While she slept, her niece was on a lookout for any trace of people
who might be fishing in the area. She noticed a movement at the
mouth of the river, wondering what it was. She couldn't ask her aunt
right away because she was still asleep in the warm weather. Finally,
her aunt woke up. The niece said, "*Senǫ*, my auntie, I've spotted something moving at the mouth of the river. It's darker in colour and bigger
in size than a swan. It keeps moving back and forth. I wonder what it is?"

"*Bebaa*, my niece," her aunt said. "A long time ago people used to come to this place to harpoon the pikes that would come out when the water starts running. It must be pikes moving."

So the aunt and her niece started walking down the ridge toward the mouth of the river where the black dot was moving. When they got out on the ice they noticed it was actually a person fishing! They walked toward him and saw that he was a man from the tribe in that area. He had many harpooned pike piled up beside him. They told him what had happened to them and where they were coming from. The man said, "Let's go back to my camp and we'll talk more about it." They all set off for the camp together.

When they got to the camp, there were lots of friendly people there, and the aunt and her niece ended up staying with them all summer. The tribe treated them kindly, just as one of their own. The aunt was still healthy and a good worker, so soon one of the tribe men wanted her for a wife. She said yes. Her niece said, "But *seno̜*, I want to go home to my people!" Her aunt told her, "It's okay for you to go home. But I will stay here with my husband now. I can't walk that far anymore, and here I have somebody to take care of me. Go ahead, and don't worry about me."

So the niece started preparing herself for the long trip home. Her aunt told her the landscape and different formations of the place so she could find her way back more easily. There would be rivers to cross, maybe dozens of them, her aunt told her. "It will probably take many, many days until you reach the big river that you need to follow. The river is called *qua-da-lee*. Then you will meet another river called *tah-ga-ra-lee*, and further up you will meet another river called Begáhdé. From there, there is a ridge on your left side and Begáhdé runs on your right side. If you follow that river," her aunt told her, "it will take you home."

Early the next morning the niece got up. She said her goodbyes to her aunt and disappeared into the wilderness. She spent days and nights travelling, meeting all the rivers, landscapes, and ridges her aunt told her she would meet. While she was travelling, she came upon a dead moose, freshly killed. She wondered where it had come from, but she decided to stay around to make drymeat and tan moosehide, which took her about a week.

Then she started moving again. The meat, being dried, was much lighter for her to pack than fresh meat. She kept on travelling, resting, and camping, following her aunt's directions. At one point, she came to a river she had to cross. She looked around and found a big spruce tree, took the bark off in one whole piece, and had an instant spruce-bark canoe. Once she crossed the river in the canoe, she overturned it and left it there. She was walking along the riverbank when she saw footprints on the sand. She wondered where they came from. Her aunt had told her that there would be a trail nearby that she should follow. She looked for it and eventually found it.

While following the trail, she spotted moose snares here and there. After a while she came to a fish lake close to the river called Taʔále and another lake called Kweteniα. As she was walking along the trail, she spotted a teepee with smoke coming out of it. She decided not to get any closer but sat down and watched. She noticed a boy playing outside with his bow and arrows. She looked and looked—was it her baby brother who stayed with her parents when she was kidnapped so many years ago? When the boy got a little closer to her, still playing with his arrows, she spoke out. "*Bechile*, younger brother, come here! I'm your long lost sister!"

Her little brother recognized his sister and ran back to the teepee to tell his parents. When he told them the good news, his parents told him that he must be wrong—his sisters were killed a long time ago by the Nahʔane people. But the little brother insisted that he just saw his older sister outside in the bushes. Finally, they all went out to see who was there. The little brother led them to where his sister was sitting. There was the daughter they thought had been killed in the war so long ago, just sitting there in the bushes, drymeat and all! The family was reunited through her bravery and the survival skills they had taught her so well.

This is a true story told by the Shúhtaot'ine people, the ancestors of Johnny Neyelle.

A Man and His Mother
Turn to Cannibalism

DURING THE TIME WHEN THE WORLD WAS NEW, around
the time when the first muzzle-loader gun came out—maybe around
1700—there was a man who was a very strong medicine man.

In those times, people would often curse each other and put hexes
on each other if they got really angry. There was one such man who
was a jealous type, and he would make his enemies dream that he was
a giant who ate people. After a while he started to believe the dream
himself and then he started hunting people and eating them. He ate
all his children and his whole family except for his mother, who also
turned to cannibalism. Everyone around was afraid of these two cannibals and started to run away to escape them, going into the mountains
or wherever they could to hide. It was during the summer that people
usually escaped the cannibals, so they wouldn't leave any footprints or
other tracks that would reveal where they had gone.

It was during this same time that the two brothers were on the
run, hiding from their enemies and making camp where no one would
find them. They lived by hunting and fishing and using snares to catch

animals, because those things didn't make noise like hunting with a muzzle-loader.

As the winter set in, they were always alert for signs of strangers and made sure to keep a close eye on each other. As winter went on, they kind of moved around, going to places where there was lots of rabbit. They knew that sooner or later the cannibals would probably find them, so they always made sure to find out where those cannibals were at any time. The two cannibals were patrolling all over the territory, looking for tracks and other signs that would tell them where there was game—that is, humans—they could kill and eat.

One morning the two brothers woke up early to check their snares. They went together down a trail using their snowshoes, but at a fork in the trail they split up, each one going a different way. They both had a muzzle-loader, though, so they felt fairly safe.

When the younger brother was at the end of his snare line, picking up a few rabbits, he turned back and noticed that his older brother was still on the snare line back at the fork. He was walking very slowly back home in his snowshoes, always on alert, looking for signs of other people. As the younger brother headed back toward the camp, he could see two shapes outside their teepee—two pairs of snowshoes. He became frightened and started hiding behind the bigger trees, moving from one to another as he approached the teepee.

All of a sudden, a shot rang out and a bullet hit him in the side, but luckily it only grazed the skin. He fell down but hung on tight to his muzzle-loader. Out of the teepee a big man with a gun came running, and the younger brother aimed and pulled the trigger and shot him. He fell down in front of the teepee.

Then a woman emerged who yelled, "You shot my son!" She screamed and ran at the younger brother with a hatchet in her hands. The younger brother started to load the muzzle-loader as fast as he could. The woman wasn't wearing her snowshoes and kept falling through the snow, a little bit every step, which slowed her down and gave the younger brother just enough time to load the gun and shoot the old woman. She dropped right in front of him.

The older brother was still walking back to the camp. He had just noticed that the younger brother had already gone back past the fork in the trail, in the direction of the teepee, when a shot rang out. He started running and heard another shot and another, all the time thinking the worst had happened to his younger brother.

As he got closer to the camp, he saw his brother sleeping by the trail, with a little blood on his side but clearly still breathing. There was a woman in front of him, dead, and a dead man in front of the teepee. His younger brother was just waking up now. The older brother didn't trust the cannibals at all. He told his brother to wait as he went to check their snowshoe tracks, because if there were more than two sets of tracks there would be more cannibals. The older brother went around to the other side of the teepee and saw only two sets of snowshoe prints in the snow. Then he knew there were no more of them. He picked up his younger brother and they moved on to another camp, leaving the two dead cannibals behind.

The older brother built a new teepee and helped his brother as he recovered from his wound. After a while he went back to where the two dead cannibals were and covered them with brush and branches. Then he went back to the teepee. As winter went on, the younger brother slowly recovered from his wound completely and started setting his snares again.

One morning, as the two brothers were sitting inside their teepee, someone started talking outside. They grabbed their guns right away and said, "Who is it?" A woman answered, saying, "Don't worry, it's just me and I know about the cannibals. I was on the run from them, but I saw they have been killed and their bodies are back there!" The older brother, always cautious, asked her to wait while he checked her snowshoe prints to make sure she was telling the truth. Then he went back to check on the dead bodies of the cannibals. After that he went to the old teepee where the cannibals had stayed, where he found the canni-bals' packsacks all stuffed with human body parts. He burned the teepee and went back home.

These were some of the stories my father used to tell us about the times when a lot of people died not of natural causes but from violence.

THERE WAS ONCE A STRONG BUT EVIL medicine man who was feared by all the people because he would kill anyone who crossed him with his medicine powers. Only two brothers who were raised by their grandmother and were in their prime young years were willing to challenge the evil medicine man and see if they could get rid of him.

The oldest brother said to the younger one, "I'll see if I can do it." He used his powers to make a spirit ghost and sent it to haunt the evil medicine man. The evil medicine man was sleeping when he saw the ghost moving around, hiding here and there. He tried to capture the ghost and destroy it, but that was hard because the oldest brother used his medicine powers to create it. Every night the ghost pushed against the evil medicine man, moving him farther and farther away from where he was sleeping.

Once he was very far away from his protected place, the oldest brother went to where the medicine man was sleeping and cut off his arms and legs. This was easily done while the medicine man was distracted in another world, trying to chase down the spirit ghost. Using his medicine powers, the oldest brother then made a big cavernous hole in the ground. In the middle of the hole he made a mound, and he placed the medicine man's arms and legs on it. He left the rest of the body on the mainland, lying there with no legs or arms, and then he made a powerful line around it using *įk'ǫzhįné*. The medicine man would never be able to pass this line and it would make him suffer and cry every time he tried.

When the evil medicine man was coming back from chasing the ghost, he saw that his arms and legs were missing. He knew right away who had done it, but he needed to recover his limbs before he could take his revenge. Once he located his arms and legs, he tried to get them back, but he couldn't take them from the mound where the oldest brother had put them because the oldest brother used strong medicine powers the evil man could not deal with.

The evil medicine man went again and again to his body, right up to the *įk'ǫzhįné* line, and cried for his arms and legs. The oldest brother had what he wanted: he wanted that medicine man to suffer because he had treated people so badly. There was nothing the evil medicine man could do. He would drag his body to the edge of the line and cry, cry, cry for his lost body parts that were sitting on the mound in the centre of the cavernous hole. And that was how he died. The oldest brother had finally killed the evil medicine man who had made the people tremble with fear.

The evil man went to the world of the spirits when he died, but he was not at rest. He wanted revenge on the person who had caused him pain and death, so he started to come back from the ghost world and try to get rid of the oldest brother who had done this to him. The oldest brother knew what the evil medicine man was trying, but he had very strong medicine powers so he wasn't that worried about himself. The evil medicine man's ghost understood how strong the oldest brother was, so he turned instead on the younger brother.

One day, the youngest brother went out hunting, looking for game, and got himself a moose with his bow and arrow. While he was skinning the moose, the evil medicine man's ghost was stalking him, but he could not see that. All of a sudden, the evil medicine man's ghost

Johnny Neyelle butchering a moose, circa 1985.

shot an arrow right through the younger brother's heart. The younger brother fell over with blood streaming from his chest and his mouth.

When the older brother came back from his hunting, he realized his brother was still gone and knew something was wrong. The very next day he went after his younger brother to see what had happened. After following the younger brother's snowshoe tracks for a long time, he came upon his brother lying on top of the moose he had killed, frozen solid already with blood coming from his mouth. The oldest brother knew at once who had done this. "I will get my revenge yet," he thought as he stood next to his brother's dead body, "and this time around I will make sure the evil medicine man never returns."

The oldest brother told his people to pack up, and together they all moved to where the younger brother lay dead. The oldest brother set up a good teepee made out of caribou skin and brought in his brother's frozen body. He said to his people, "Do not try to wake me up or even come near my teepee when I'm asleep, because there is lots of medicine power being used." He pushed his brother's frozen body into his rabbit-skin blanket and he went to sleep. In his sleep, he saw right away where his younger brother had been stalked and killed by the evil medicine man. He could also see the path on which the evil medicine man had taken the younger brother back to the ghost world.

The oldest brother started following the trail they left. He watched the land around him change as he got closer and closer to the ghost world. When he got to the land of the ghosts, he couldn't go in. He had to stay outside and watch from a distance, trying to locate his brother among the other ghosts. Finally, he saw him. He signalled to his brother to come closer as he tried to figure out how to bring him back to his body. Since he couldn't touch his brother in that ghost world, he decided to make a rope out of moose skin.

He tied one end around his waist and then with the other end he lassoed his younger brother around the waist. Together, they started back toward the living world. The ground around the teepee where their bodies lay began to shake and crumble as they got closer. Once they reached their bodies, the older brother removed the arrow from his younger brother's frozen body and he let his brother's spirit move back into place. Soon they both stood up, awakening from the ghost world.

The oldest brother said, "I must work my medicine power on the evil medicine man so he cannot come back and hurt us ever again." He asked his people if they had a large stone he could use in making his medicine power against the evil medicine man's spirit in the ghost world. The people looked around and gave him one.

The oldest brother lay a white caribou hide down on the ground and placed the white stone on it. Then he placed another white caribou hide over top. He and his younger brother started chanting and singing on the stone that was sitting between the hides. Soon it started to grow bigger and bigger, until it turned into a giant grizzly bear. Then the oldest brother said, "I also need something like a dog to follow the bear and bark." The people brought him a small dog, which he killed. Then he sent the bear and the dog into the spirit world, following the scent trail that the evil medicine man's ghost had left behind.

The evil medicine man was among the other ghosts in the crowded land of the dead when he heard a dog barking and coming toward him. He took out his bow and arrow to shoot the threatening dog and, when he was distracted, the giant grizzly bear took his opportunity to attack. The bear pounced on the evil medicine man. The man tried to turn and shoot the bear, but his arrows just bounced off because of the hard stone from which the bear was made. The giant bear kept after the medicine man, who kept trying to shoot him and to run away and escape. But in the end the bear got the evil medicine man in his jaws.

All this time the oldest brother was narrating what was happening in the spirit world to his people in the real world. He said, "Because of what the evil medicine man has done to the people here, I will make sure he doesn't return ever again." He used his strong medicine powers to push the bear, with the evil medicine man in its jaws, into the second ghost land. That ended the evil medicine man's attempts at revenge. The people did not have any more problems with the evil medicine man. They never heard from him again, ever.

Tł'o-k'áe-tee, the Medicine Man

THERE ONCE WAS A MAN NAMED TŁ'O-K'ÁE-TEE, which means willow grass. He was a strong, very gifted medicine man. Once a spirit from the underworld decided to kidnap Tł'o-k'áe-tee's wife. Tł'o-k'áe-tee could tell ahead of time that this would happen, as his medicine powers let him know these things. It didn't bother him that much, since both he and his wife were always loners and didn't associate with anybody else, but it stayed on his mind.

One day, Tł'o-k'áe-tee was out hunting. When he returned home, he found his wife lying on the ground, dead. He knew that it was a spirit from the underworld who had done this, a spirit who had come to take his wife back to the land of the spirits. Tł'o-k'áe-tee knew immediately where they had gone, and he decided to use his medicine powers to try to get his wife back. He took his wife's dead body and a woven rabbit blanket into his bed with him, and went to sleep.

That night, when he was in the dream world, he saw a whole tribe of spirits. They were the ones who had kidnapped his wife and taken her to their world. In the dream world, Tł'o-k'áe-tee started following the spirits' trail.

All along the way he saw willows pulled out from the ground. These were what his wife had tried to grab hold of to get away from the spirits, but they had kept on dragging her along. The trail led Tłʼo-kʼáe-tee to a river, and there he couldn't tell which way the spirits had gone, upriver or downriver. Then he noticed air bubbles coming out downriver and knew that's where they were. He turned and continued on. On and on he went until the land itself started to change colour around him. It was becoming a reddish evil colour—a colour of a land where only weird beings could live, he thought.

He soon came upon a calm river entering a lake. At the very end of the lake he spied a fish trap and thought it must belong to the spirits who had taken his wife. He realized he would not be able to make it across the water in his human form, so he transformed into *tłʼo kʼáe*, a willow grass, and drifted on the water toward the fish trap. Once he had drifted into it, he stopped and floated there for a while, waiting to see what would happen.

Soon a woman came toward the lake carrying a spruce-bark bucket, intending to gather water. She looked into the fish trap and saw the single willow grass branch floating there. "That's strange," she thought. She picked it up and looked at it for a moment, then dropped it back in the fish trap. She took her spruce bucket and filled it with water, then continued on her way back to her village. Tłʼo-kʼáe-tee quickly transformed back into his human form and followed her.

The woman went into a hut that was built partway underground, like a small cave. Tłʼo-kʼáe-tee went to the entrance of the hut and listened. She was talking to her elderly parents. "Father," she asked, "why is it that I saw a *tłʼo kʼáe*, a willow grass, floating in the fish trap?" Her father replied, "Eh, eh, that was what I was talking about! Tłʼo-kʼáe-tee, the strongest and most powerful medicine man ever, and you wanted to kidnap his wife! Well, that's him for sure." The father turned away, not feeling too good at all.

Very soon, Tłʼo-kʼáe-tee entered the hut. The people saw him as a stranger and welcomed him, asking him to please sit close to the fire.

So that was where Tłʼo-kʼáe-tee sat. The eldest woman dug behind some shrubs and brought out a freshly caught whitefish, which she placed on the open fire to roast. When it was well cooked all the way through, she put the cooked fish on a spruce-bark tray and presented it to Tłʼo-kʼáe-tee. "Stranger, this is the only kind of food we eat," she said. "Please enjoy your meal." Tłʼo-kʼáe-tee picked up the fish and swallowed the whole thing at once.

Then they heard noises outside the hut, laughter and water splashing. The old man said, "Those must be the young men playing and showing off for the women." Tłʼo-kʼáe-tee got up, saying he would like to see what kind of games the young people were playing, and he went out of the hut. He walked toward the young people in the water. Among them he could see one who was really an otter in human form, playing along with the rest, swimming, diving, and laughing.

He also saw his wife. Tłʼo-kʼáe-tee had finally caught up with his wife's kidnappers. He didn't say anything for a while, just watched them having fun together. One young man said to him, "Hey stranger! We're just having fun here, come join us if you like!" But Tłʼo-kʼáe-tee replied, "No, I'm just here to watch." The young people kept on playing. Tłʼo-kʼáe-tee watched one of them demonstrate his magic powers by pulling on his arm, releasing some kind of bright rays that bounced off the water and returned to him.

After he was finished, it was the women's turn to show their powers. One of the women threw her powers far across the river; they bounced and created a beautiful rainbow arcing over the whole river, then bounced back to her. Everyone was very entertained.

One of the young men said to Tłʼo-kʼáe-tee, "Hey stranger! Why don't you show us your magic powers too? If you have any!" Everyone laughed when he said that. Tłʼo-kʼáe-tee said calmly, "I don't know how." But they kept teasing him in front of the beautiful women until finally he had enough of that taunting. He said, "Fine, I will play for you" and pulled on his wrist to let out the powers of the sun's rays that were hidden there. The sunlight splashed across the river and returned to him just like magic.

While everyone was watching the sun's rays play on the river, Tłʼo-kʼáe-tee turned to his wife. "Grab my waist and hold on tight," he said, "and don't let go until I say so!" Tłʼo-kʼáe-tee pulled his wrist even harder and the sun's rays started to get hotter and hotter on the river until the water started to boil. The spirits of the underworld who were in the river were boiled alive. The spirits who were still on the land got so hot they tried to get relief from their anguish by jumping into the river, but it boiled them alive too.

Tłʼo-kʼáe-tee let his powers fade as soon as he could tell they were all dead. The river cooled down quickly back to its normal temperature. He and his wife were both fine because it was Tłʼo-kʼáe-tee's medicine—it didn't hurt him, and his wife had held onto him so she wasn't hurt either. Tłʼo-kʼáe-tee told his wife to point the way, to retrace the trail the kidnappers had used when they took her. They followed the trail together all the way back to the teepee where they were sleeping in their own world.

Tłʼo-kʼáe-tee awakened. He said to his wife, "Get up! Wake up and make a fire! What did you go and get lost in the other world for?" She got up and made fire. Tłʼo-kʼáe-tee shook his head. He thought about what he had done to the spirit-world kidnappers. He was sure they had learned their lesson and they would not cause any such problems again. Tłʼo-kʼáe-tee and his wife lived well forever after that.

This is one of the stories that was passed on to us during the cold winter nights when there wasn't much to do.

Yamorehya, the One Who Walked the World

IN THE TIME OF THE DINOSAURS, dinosaurs used to roam the countryside feeding on humans. *Náhʑácho* was the name that was given to the dinosaurs, which came in all types: giant birds and all other species of animal. At that time, people would often go out into the world and never come back. They were all killed and eaten by the giant dinosaurs. Two brothers who were raised by their grandmother said they would try to solve these and other problems, so they went out into the world to see what they could do. The older brother's name was Yamorehya, and this is his story.

When the two brothers became adults, they started travelling the world to see if they could help people in many different places. Their grandmother gave them her blessing before they left. Then they were off on their journeys to solve the problems of the world. Soon after they had set out, they passed through a rocky, rugged countryside where they came upon a couple of Elders who seemed to be very kind and who offered them food and shelter.

The old Elders were living in a cave. They put the two brothers in the far end of the cave, saying, "You two must be very tired. Rest while we get the fire going." They built the fire up high and then they kept on throwing more and more kindling and wood on it, until the fire got so hot the two brothers could hardly breathe. They began to fear they would be cooked alive if they stayed in the cave any longer. But they were trapped in the far end of the cave by the fire and couldn't get out.

The younger brother started yelling at Yamorehya, saying, "I can't breathe! We're not going to make it!" But Yamorehya said, "Wait, I will see what I can do with my powers." He summoned up his medicine power and directed it at the fiery cave. Soon they could hear water, like the gurgling of a river.

Suddenly out of the fire came a burst of water, which shot across the cave toward the old couple of Elders, who were waiting for the two brothers to be cooked alive so they could eat them. Those two cannibals drowned in the water that drenched them, and that was the end of them. That was the two brothers' first experience with the problems of the world that they had set out to face together, and there would be many more dangerous ones to come.

After their experience with the cannibals, the brothers continued on, always expecting the unexpected. They didn't trust anyone and were always prepared for battle. They roamed all over the world, spending a night here and there. They kept moving until they came to a place where many dinosaurs and other giant human-eating creatures came from. Those creatures went out into the world from here and caused problems for people everywhere.

Yamorehya said to his brother, "Brother, I will travel toward where the sun rises and you will go toward where the sun sets, and we will both do whatever it takes to fix this problem of the human-eating creatures." With that, the brothers went their separate ways.

Yamorehya continued on by himself and soon came upon a trail that looked like it had been used a lot. It was a very rocky trail that cut through a dense forest with big giant trees, thick with willows. Yamorehya checked carefully to see if there were any traps or snares around that could catch him. Now he was always alert and on the lookout for those things. He didn't see anything threatening, but then, without warning, a snare caught him by the neck and hung him up! There was a string of human bones still caught in the snare and they tangled with the snare rope to bind Yamorehya tight.

Yamorehya dangled in the snare, unable to reach any of his tools to cut himself free. Then he thought about his medicine powers and how he could use them to get loose. He summoned up a beaver tooth, which snipped the snare that was wound around his neck. He fell down from the snare and all the human bones fell on top of him, but he wasn't injured.

Yamorehya kept walking along this unknown trail that had already nearly done him in. He had all sorts of fighting weapons with him, like bow and arrow, stone axe, club, and razor-like knives made of special stones, so he was well prepared to fight whatever he would face.

As he continued walking, he saw a strange sort of human walking toward him. It was one of the Ɂemǫ́ǫhdzí, lion people, who was checking his snares to see if he had caught any humans to eat. That was how the lion people hunted and survived. The Ɂemǫ́ǫhdzí said to Yamorehya with surprise, "Stranger, how did you get there? How did you get past my snares?" Yamorehya lied to the Ɂemǫ́ǫhdzí, saying, "No, grandpa, I only got on the trail not too far from here and I haven't been on it long." The lion person said, "There's no way you got past my snares. You're lying!" and he attacked Yamorehya.

Yamorehya jumped from rock to rock along the trail and dodged the lion person's grasp. He started shooting it with his arrows, but they had no effect—they just bounced off or shattered against the lion person's tough hide. How could he make his arrows pierce this Ɂemǫ́ǫhdzí, Yamorehya asked himself, as he jumped from rock to rock running away from the great creature. Then he got an idea and took up another arrow. He aimed at the bottom of the lion person's neck, the softest place he could think of, and let go. Sure enough, the arrow went through the skin and pierced the lion person with a deadly wound. The Ɂemǫ́ǫhdzí fell to the ground, dead.

Yamorehya continued along the trail and soon met another ʔemǫ́ǫhdzí, the wife of the first one he had killed. This one said to Yamorehya, "Hey stranger, I was following your grandpa down this trail. Have you seen him?" Again Yamorehya lied, saying, "No, I haven't seen grandpa because I just got on this trail a little while back." The lion person's wife said, "How can it be that you didn't see him? This is the only trail that leads this way!" And with that she attacked Yamorehya.

But Yamorehya jumped easily out of the way. This time he knew what to do: he aimed his arrow at the bottom of the lion's neck and let go. The ʔemǫ́ǫhdzí wife fell to the ground, dead at his feet. Yamorehya knew that these ʔemǫ́ǫhdzí were the only ones of their kind who ate people and that he had rid the world of a dangerous threat by killing them.

Yamorehya continued walking wherever the trail took him. Days, months, and years went by as he continued through barren lands.

One day, in the winter, Yamorehya was walking along in his snow-shoes when he spotted a very small snowshoe print in the snow. He looked around for more and found a trail of them. He started following the snowshoe prints, wondering what could have made them. There were snares set all along the path he was going down, and here and there a rabbit had been caught, but Yamorehya didn't bother with those. He just kept on going.

Finally, Yamorehya came upon a small community—that is, a community of small people, about the size of a mouse. When the mouse people saw Yamorehya, they screamed and yelled in fear for the big giant who was invading them. "Run for your lives!" they screamed. Yamorehya reassured them, saying, "Wait, come back! I'm a good person and I don't kill or eat people, no matter how small they are!" One by one, all the mouse people who had scattered came back, curious to see who this giant was and whether he really was not dangerous.

Yamorehya told the mouse people that he had followed their snow-shoe tracks and that along the way he saw there were some rabbits caught in snares. The mouse people were very happy. They said, "Ay, the stranger says we caught some moose with our snares!" They went back down the trail to find the rabbits, which to the mouse people were as big as moose were to Yamorehya. They butchered the rabbits and roasted the hindquarters for their guest, Yamorehya, who, to their amazement, swallowed it all in one bite. To the mouse people it was huge, but to Yamorehya it was pretty small.

Then the mouse people asked Yamorehya to come with them to trap for more moose. They walked on their snowshoes together, Yamorehya in the middle and the mouse people all spread out around him. When they got to the place where moose were hanging around, they said to Yamorehya, "We will chase the moose toward you and you can kill it for us." Then they took off a little ways into the bush.

Yamorehya stood there, waiting to see moose come out of the bush very shortly, but instead he saw two *béhdzįga*, snowy owls, coming toward him. They flew right past him up over the treetops. Soon after they passed, the mouse people came running out of the bush. "What happened?" they asked. "Where is the moose that came this way?" Yamorehya was surprised. "But I didn't see any moose," he said. "The only thing I saw was two snowy owls."

The mouse people started to head back to the camp, disappointed. Yamorehya thought for a minute and realized they were talking about the *béhdzįga*, which, like the rabbit, they were calling moose. He went after the owls in the direction they had flown. Soon he saw the two *béhdzįga* perched up in a tree. He got out his bow and arrows and got them both with one shot. He plucked their feathers and roasted one of them over a fire for himself to eat, remembering how good *béhdzįga* taste, like spruce grouse. After having a good meal, he got up and hooked the other *béhdzįga* on the side of his moosehide belt to carry back with him to the mouse people.

When he got back, the mouse people were huddled around their fire, very hungry. He threw down the owl and they jumped up happily, saying, "Ay, the stranger has killed a moose for us!" They tried to drag the owl over to the fire, but its head alone was too heavy for them. Yamorehya grabbed the owl and moved it over to where the mouse people could start butchering it. Yamorehya was tired then, so he went back to his own caribou teepee and rested while the mouse people butchered, cooked, and ate the *béhdzįga*, which they called moose.

Yamorehya could hear something being sawed while he was in the teepee. Soon one of the women came to him and offered him the beak of the snowy owl. "Stanger," she said, "we give this special food to the one who is a good hunter." Yamorehya was disgusted because he didn't eat that part of the owl. He threw it away, thinking to himself, "What would I do with a piece of bone?" But the mouse people scavenged for the beak and shared it among themselves—that was the kind of people they were.

Yamorehya stayed with the mouse people for years, and after a time they gave him one of their daughters to stay with him. Yamorehya treated her well and raised her up to the size of a muskrat. When summer came again one year, Yamorehya went hunting for his kind of moose. He got one with his bow and arrow and butchered it. Then he went back to camp and told his mouse people about it. They had no idea what kind of moose he was talking about, so they wanted to go with him to see for themselves. They followed a rough trail marked with moss Yamorehya had strung on willow branches until they came to the place where he had killed the moose.

Yamorehya's father-in-law, the father of his muskrat-sized wife, ran ahead because he was so curious. Suddenly, he shouted and ran back toward the group. "Ay, it's the monster I had to save my kids from when they fell into its footprints!" he yelled. "Stay away from there—go back home!" The father ran all the way back to the camp. His family was afraid too, but they thought that if the stranger Yamorehya knew this kind of moose, it should be fine.

When Yamorehya and everyone else retuned to the camp, Yamorehya took the moose's head and hung it by the fire to roast. His father-in-law was watching cautiously from his own teepee. After a while the father-in-law was tempted by the smell of the moose head cooking. He said to his wife, "I think I'll go over and visit my son-in-law. Smells like he's cooking something." He went over and sat near the fire to take a look at what it was. To him, the moose head just looked like a giant piece of bone.

He went back over to his wife and said, "Well, I thought he was cooking something to eat, but it's just a piece of bone. Why don't you cook up that snowy owl's beak instead?" The wife had started to get the beak ready when Yamorehya stopped in to present a big bowl of the cut-up moose head, with eyeballs still on it, to his father-in-law. The father-in-law was skeptical, but Yamorehya said, "Even though you may think it's just bones, try to eat it and see if you like it."

His father-in-law jumped into the bowl and started eating, crawling around inside the eye sockets and eating every little piece of fat on the skull. Because he was so small, he could get every tiny piece there was, nibbling and nibbling as he searched for more. Finally, he was so full he stopped, saying to his wife, "I thought it was just bones, but there was so much fat there it made me dizzy!"

As the years went by the mouse people appreciated how much bigger the daughter had gotten who was given to Yamorehya. They decided to give him another wife since he was so good at raising the first one. But Yamorehya said, "No, I can't accept another wife because I have to move on soon. I never stay in one place that long." Soon after that, he left the mouse people and his mouse wife, setting out into the world again to see what would come next.

Yamorehya was roaming around the country of the dinosaurs and cannibals when he came upon a man, his wife, and their daughter living all by themselves. They said, "Ay, stranger, come for a visit! Don't be afraid, we're good people and that's who we are." The parents were elderly people who kept a giant dinosaur as a pet, feeding it unsuspecting humans who came by. Yamorehya didn't know that yet, but he soon would, and, after all, it was his job to straighten out people who lived that way.

Right away the elderly couple gave Yamorehya their daughter to be his wife so that he would stay long enough for them to trap him. He accepted and they lived together for a while, Yamorehya going out to hunt and gather food for them all. But Yamorehya could tell there was something not right about the people he was living with now.

One day, Yamorehya needed to make himself some more arrows, but he didn't have any more feathers, spruce gum, sinew, arrowheads, or really any of the things he needed. He asked his wife to see if her father had any feathers he could use to make his arrows. The elderly man came out of his teepee and pointed to the west. He said to his son-in-law, Yamorehya, "Just go toward where the sun sets. That's where I always get my feathers, and that's where you should go."

There was a path leading toward the setting sun, which was the one on which the old man would send the humans who visited him to meet the dinosaur and their death. Yamorehya packed up his hunting gear and his weapons and started on the path the old man had pointed out, wondering what he would face.

Yamorehya spent days and weeks on the path, looking for the good place to find feathers. As he was walking among some very tall trees, he saw an eagle's nest way up top. He knew that had to be the place. He climbed up to the nest and found two young eagles there. Yamorehya started talking to them, asking, "Where are your parents?" They answered that their parents were out hunting. Back in the days of the dinosaurs, humans and animals could understand each other. So Yamorehya said, "Which one of you is going to rat on me when your parents get back?" The female baby eagle said, "I will tell my parents you were here when they get back," so Yamorehya grabbed her and clubbed her to death and threw her over the side of the nest.

Then he said to the male baby eagle, "What about you? Will you also tell on me?" "No, no, no," said the young eagle, "I will not tell on you!" Yamorehya asked the young eagle when his parents were coming back, and what would let him know they were coming. The young eagle told him that once his father had started on his way home it would start snowing a wet snow and drizzle. "That's how I always know my father is returning," he said. "And what about your mother?" Yamorehya asked. "When my mother is on her flight home," replied the young eagle, "it will start to hail and get really windy."

"What do your parents bring back for food?" Yamorehya asked next. "Sometimes they bring back moose, sheep, and other animals like that," the young eagle told him. "But sometimes they bring back human remains." "I see," said Yamorehya. Then he said to the young eagle, "When your father comes back, he will ask you where your sister is. You will answer him by saying that your sister has a headache because it is too warm, so she went down from the nest to cool off. Your father will ask you why he can smell humans. You will say it's just the scent of the human remains he brought back. When your father double-checks around the nest for any humans, I will club him to death."

When it started to snow wet snow, Yamorehya knew the father eagle was on his way back to the nest. He told the young one that he was going to hide behind the trunk of the tree and get ready, which he did. The father eagle soon arrived at the nest, carrying half a moose and half a human in each claw. The father eagle said to the young one, "Where is your sister?" "She went down to cool off," said the young eagle. "She had a headache." The father eagle twitched his beak. "Why can I smell humans?" he said. "Oh, that must be the smell of the human you just brought back," replied the young eagle.

The father was suspicious and took flight again, circling the nest to see if any humans were around. As he passed Yamorehya near the ground, Yamorehya took a mighty swing with his club and hit the eagle hard, killing him and sending his body spiralling toward the ground. Yamorehya climbed back up to the nest. He said to the young eagle, "This human your father brought you to eat is no good for you. You should not live your life the way your father did, killing humans." He threw the human remains out of the nest and took a piece of fat from the moose to feed to the young eagle.

Then he said to the eagle, "When your mother comes back, tell her what I just told you. She will wonder where your father is because he usually comes home first. Then your mother will ask you why she can smell humans. You will tell her the same thing you told your father. When your mother double-checks around the nest for any humans, I will club her to death."

When the mother eagle returned, everything happened the way Yamorehya said. He killed the mother eagle the same way he killed the father eagle. Then he threw the human remains the mother had brought back over the side of the nest, and took another small piece of moose fat to feed the young eagle.

The young eagle said to Yamorehya, "How will I survive, now that you killed both my parents?" "You will do fine alone," Yamorehya replied. "You will live by eating the meat, moose and other kinds, that is left over by hunters. But you will never eat human flesh again, as long as you live."

Then Yamorehya asked the young eagle to wait in the nest while he climbed down. Once Yamorehya was on the ground, he busied himself in a small pond near the base of the tree. The eagle couldn't see what he was doing and was interested to know what was going on. Eventually, Yamorehya called out to the eagle, "I've made a fish to swim near the surface of this little pond. Can you see it?" The eagle peered over the edge of the nest. "Yes, I can see it," he said. Yamorehya said, "Good. Now dive from the nest as fast as you can. When you reach the pond, dip your beak in and grab the fish." The young eagle tried it and he was good at it right away. He caught the fish in his mouth and ate it up. So, to this day, you can still see eagles diving for fish and snatching them out of the water.

Yamorehya collected all the feathers he needed and started on the long walk home. When he returned, he started working on his arrows again, but soon he needed sinews to tie the feathers in place. He asked his wife to see if her father had any sinews he could use. His father-in-law came out of his teepee and said to his son-in-law, Yamorehya,

"Just go south, toward the warm country. That's where I always get my sinews, and that's where you should go."

Yamorehya knew the old man was trying to kill him, sending him again on a dangerous path toward giants or dinosaurs or cannibals. But he also knew that it was his job to rid the world of such beings. So he gathered up his weapons and went in the direction his father-in-law had indicated, wondering what he would face this time.

He walked for days and weeks before he reached a clearing with no trees. He saw a giant *gokw'i ejiré*, a muskox, lying there with a big sandpiper nest on top of its horn. The sandpiper was like a lookout for the muskox: as soon as it saw Yamorehya, it started piping a distress signal to the muskox. But Yamorehya made a hand gesture that stopped the sandpiper short. The sleeping muskox opened one eye and said to the sandpiper, "What's all this? You made a noise and woke me up." The sandpiper was under Yamorehya's influence, and he replied, "I'm sorry, I thought something was moving, but it was just some light flickering off a leaf."

Yamorehya thought this big muskox must be the creature his father-in-law had sent him toward. He thought about how to get close to it without being in danger, and he had an idea. With his powers, Yamorehya concentrated on the shape of a mouse. Very soon a mouse showed up.

"I need your help," Yamorehya said to the mouse. "I want you to go underground and build a tunnel that leads straight to the ox's heart. Make room in the tunnel for my bow and arrow too. That's how I can get a shot at it." The mouse said, "Sure, I can do that." Yamorehya instructed the mouse, "When you scrape away the earth near the muskox, it will scrape away some of his hair. He will be startled and say, 'What is that bugging me from underneath?' and you should say, 'Oh grandpa, I'm just getting some of your hair to line my nest so my family can sleep well through the cold winter.'"

The mouse nodded and right away went underground to begin to make the tunnel. He did just what Yamorehya told him to do. When he got to the heart area, where the great muscle was thumping so loudly, he started scraping the hair away. The giant *gokw'i ejiré* woke up and said, "What is that bugging me from underneath?" and the mouse replied, "Oh it's only me, grandpa, collecting some hair for my family so they can sleep well on cold winter nights." The muskox went back to sleep. The mouse finished his job and came back up out of the tunnel he had made. "Yamorehya, I did what you told me," he said, "and everything is ready."

Yamorehya made himself as small as a mouse and entered the tunnel. He got right underneath the heart of the sleeping muskox, so close he could feel it pumping, *thump, thump, thump.* Yamorehya took out his bow and arrow and aimed at the huge thumping heart. He let his arrow fly. Then he hurried away to a deep part of the tunnel, moving fast so the muskox couldn't hurt him.

The muskox let out a loud roar as the arrow pierced his heart. He cried, "Sandpiper, why did you lie to me? You said it was only a flickering leaf!" and he thrashed around, trying to get at the sandpiper. Yamorehya hid in his corner of the tunnel until all the thrashing and roaring and shaking of the ground finally stopped. He came out of the tunnel to see the giant *gokw'i ejiré* lying dead on the ground, an arrow through its heart. Yamorehya thanked the mouse for the work he had done. Then he butchered the giant muskox and took all the sinew he wanted.

Yamorehya started walking back home. It took him days and days to get back using a safe path that avoided giants and dinosaurs. When he finally got home, Yamorehya set to work on his arrows again. He got the feathers in place and used the sinew to tie them down. But now he needed spruce gum and an arrowhead to finish everything off. He asked his wife to see if her father had any spruce gum he could use. The old man pointed far away to the east and said to Yamorehya, "Just go toward where the sun rises. That's where I always get my spruce gum, and that's where you should go."

Yamorehya gathered his things and once again set out walking. It was days and weeks until he saw anyone. The creature he saw was making a lot of noise at the side of a steep cliff. Yamorehya came closer and saw that it was a *nǫgha*, a male wolverine. The wolverine kept running back and forth from the edge of the cliff, looking down and then running back in excitement.

When he saw Yamorehya, he said, "Hey stranger, there's a whole herd of sheep just over the side of this cliff." Yamorehya got closer, and the wolverine nudged him toward the cliff's edge. All of a sudden, the wolverine pushed Yamorehya over the edge. He started to fall down the chasm toward a ground covered with spikes, but he used his powers to turn himself into a feather, which floated gently to the bottom without being torn.

Yamorehya turned back into himself once he had landed safely and looked around to see that it was a bone trap: the spikes were sharp human shin bones driven into the ground everywhere, meant to impale humans who fell over the edge of the cliff. Yamorehya knew the wolverine was trying to kill him. He nicked his nose with his hunting knife and rubbed some blood over the nearby bone spikes. Then he lay down carefully on top of the spikes and pretended to be dead.

Not too long after he had closed his eyes, he heard the wolverine approaching, singing and very happy, carrying a huge packsack. The wolverine grabbed Yamorehya and tossed him into the packsack. Then the wolverine started on his way home. As they went on their way up the trail, Yamorehya would reach out of the packsack and grab hold of willow branches, making the wolverine pull harder to keep moving. The wolverine said to himself, "Boy, this is heavy—these humans sure freeze fast." When the wolverine arrived at his camp, he dropped Yamorehya at the side of a great open fire as his children rushed toward him in welcome. "We'll eat well today with some fresh meat," he told the children, who danced happily around the fire.

The wolverine then told his wife to cut up the meat and start cooking it. The wolverine's wife grabbed a wooden knife. She undid the packsack, took Yamorehya out, and starting trying to butcher his flesh. But the knife couldn't cut through Yamorehya's tough flesh. So the wife went to get a very sharp, stone-glass knife, which she was sure would work. As she approached him with the sharp knife, Yamorehya knew he had to make his move.

He thought hard about a wooden club and sure enough a wooden club appeared by his side. As the wife moved in to cut his flesh, Yamorehya grabbed the club, jumped up, and attacked. He clubbed the wolverine's wife and all of the wolverine's children, except two small ones who got away by climbing up a spruce tree. These two wolverines were crafty, and whenever Yamorehya shot arrows at them they could deflect them with gestures of their hands. Yamorehya lit a fire under the tree to see if he could smoke them out, but the young wolverines just peed on the fire and laughed at him.

Yamorehya decided to wait them out. He sat by the tree for days and weeks, waiting for the young wolverines to come down, but they stayed in the tree. Finally, one of the wolverines called down to Yamorehya, "Hey, if you let us go safely, we will give you some spruce gum." Yamorehya agreed. The young wolverines blew their noses loudly and out came a whole bunch of spruce gum, dripping down the tree. Yamorehya collected all the spruce gum he could carry and started walking away.

One of the young wolverines yelled after him, "What about us? How will we survive, now that you killed both our parents?" "You will do fine alone," Yamorehya replied. "You will live by stealing from other people, taking meat from their traps. But you will never eat human flesh again, as long as you live." To this day, that's how the wolverine survives, by stealing from others.

Yamorehya started back home. Days and weeks passed until he came home to the camp. Once he had arrived, Yamorehya went back to work on his arrows. Soon enough, he needed arrowheads to finish them. He asked his wife to see if her father had any arrowheads. The old man came out of his teepee. He pointed north and said to

Yamorehya, "Just go toward the barren lands. That's where I always get my arrowheads, and that's where you should go."

Yamorehya prepared himself once more for a long journey, wondering to himself what he would face this time. He set out on his journey, moving into colder and colder lands and spending days here and there as he continued in the direction his father-in-law had pointed out. One day, he climbed up a mountainous rock and stood on top of it, looking down into a perfectly round pond where he could see two giant frogs with their mouths wide open. They were lying in wait to swallow anything that might drop from the mountain.

Yamorehya thought to himself, "How can I kill these two giant frogs?" He thought about it for a while and eventually he started making a fire around two big boulders that were sitting on top of the mountain. He gathered a lot of dry wood and sticks for kindling and made the fire really big. It took a few days for it to get really hot. Once it was hot enough, Yamorehya got a big pole and used it to push one of the boulders over the edge of the mountain. It took a while, but then it finally started to move.

The boulder rolled down the steep edge of the mountain. The frogs sitting by the pond opened their mouths even wider, expecting food, but instead one of them swallowed the big hot boulder! The giant frog that had swallowed the boulder jumped desperately into the pond to cool off, but it was no use. The frog died almost instantly. Then Yamorehya pushed the other hot boulder over the edge of the mountain. The other giant frog swallowed it and then it also died. Yamorehya climbed down the mountain to where the frogs' bodies were lying. Scattered around were hundreds of good arrowheads. He picked up as many as he wanted.

Yamorehya started back home once again, wondering what his father- and mother-in-law were going to say about all his travels. When he arrived, he went back to work on his arrows, and at last he got them all finished. Then his parents-in-law saw him. "He's back again," they said to each other. "He must have killed all of our pets!" They asked their daughter, Yamorehya's wife, to turn into a grizzly bear and kill Yamorehya.

One afternoon, Yamorehya was wandering in a wooded area, eating berries that he found here and there, when he was attacked out of nowhere by a giant grizzly bear. He ran back to the camp with the bear behind him and, once he got close, he yelled to his father-in-law, "Get me my bow and arrow so I can kill this bear!" His father-in-law came running toward him with bow and arrows in hand and threw them to Yamorehya. Yamorehya caught them and tried to shoot the bear, even as he continued to run away. But his father-in-law had replaced all his hard-won stone arrowheads with wooden ones, which just shattered when they were fired.

Yamorehya thought fast. He remembered once seeing his father-in-law throw away some chipped arrowheads into the shrubs nearby. He headed in that direction and, sure enough, he could see arrowheads lying on the ground. He grabbed one from the ground as he ran past the small pile and stuck it as best he could to the end of his arrow. Then he aimed at the bear and let go. The giant grizzly let out a great roar as it fell to the ground, crying in his wife's voice, "Father, mother, he has killed me too!" Then she died.

Yamorehya's father- and mother-in-law were now even angrier. They came after him with heavy stone axes. Yamorehya ran from them and transformed into a beaver. He jumped into the lake. The elderly couple saw him transform and knew the beaver was really Yamorehya. "I'll go get my beaver net," the old man said, "and we'll get him after all!" The old man went and got his beaver net. He set it across a little channel and then he and his wife sat down and waited.

Yamorehya saw them waiting for him. He dove and swam around in his beaver body, wondering what to do. In order to fool them, he threw a big rock into the beaver net and then swam away. When the old man saw the rock move the net, he yelled, "We got him!" and started to pull the net out of the water. When he and his wife saw that it was just a rock, they were surprised. Then they thought that probably Yamorehya had turned himself into a rock. They started beating it with their stone axes. After a while the rock was pounded to pieces and their axe was shattered too. Then, right in front of them, that beaver stuck its head out of the water! Beaver-Yamorehya twirled around in the water and slapped his tail on the surface of the lake, teasing the old couple he had so easily fooled.

The old man didn't like that much. He told his woman, "That's enough. I'm going to go get my two dinosaurs. They will drink all the water from this lake and then we can finally kill Yamorehya." The old man went and brought his two giant, thirsty pet dinosaurs to the water's edge. They started to guzzle up all the water. As the water level got lower and lower, Yamorehya the beaver turned into a small fish fry and hid in a shallow puddle. The dinosaurs drank all the water from the lake and all the fish dried up and died. Then the old man and his wife walked among the mud puddles, searching out any remaining living things—bugs, snails, little fish, anything—and killing them all. "Don't leave anything alive," the old man said to his wife. "It could be Yamorehya." This went on for days and weeks as the old man and woman covered the whole lake.

Soon they were closing in on the puddle where Yamorehya was hiding. Yamorehya had to do something. He thought hard about a sandpiper and sure enough a sandpiper landed next to his puddle. "I need your help," Yamorehya said to the sandpiper. "Can you fly under those two giant dinosaurs and poke holes in their bellies with your sharp beak?" The sandpiper said he could do that. "Wait," said Yamorehya, "if they ask what a skinny-legged creature like you is doing underneath them, you should tell them you're just looking in the mud for bugs and snails for your young ones."

The sandpiper agreed and flew over to the giant dinosaurs, circling around them and landing every now and then in the mud beneath them. "What's that skinny-legged creature doing there beneath us?" said one of the dinosaurs to the other. "I'm just looking for bugs and snails for my young ones," the sandpiper called. Sandpiper kept pecking at the mud as if he was looking for small bugs. Then, in the blink of an eye, he flew up and pecked a little hole in each of the giant dinosaurs' bellies. Then he flew away very quickly. The giant dinosaurs felt the prick and let out little squeals. "That skinny-legged creature tricked us!" they yelled, as the water gushed out of the holes in their bellies and started filling up the lake again.

The old man and his wife were in the middle of the lake when it started to fill up again. They started running toward the shore. The old man made it in time to jump onto the dry land, but the old lady was flooded with the water and floated up. The old man grabbed a long pole and used it to fish his wife out of the lake by twisting her hair around the end. The couple sat together by the shoreline watching the lake fill up when right before their eyes that beaver popped up and slapped its tail. They knew it was Yamorehya again, but there wasn't much they could do. They just sat there, defeated.

They sat there for so long the hay grass eventually grew up around them. To this day, sometimes you can see these balls of hay grass on the lakeshores. Finally, Yamorehya had killed the two troll-like people who were sending people to their deaths in the jaws of their human-eating pets.

After that adventure, Yamorehya continued wandering the world looking for ways to make the world a better place for tomorrow. As he was travelling the world, he would deal with all the problems, big and small, that he encountered. He corrected many problems that used to plague the people and now we have a better world than before.

YAMOGAH WAS A GIANT OF A MAN. He was a very strong warrior for his people, the Shúhtaot'ine.

Yamogah and his people were wandering in the mountains one day when Yamogah was attacked by a giant grizzly bear. The bear was sent by one of the strong shamans of the Nahʔane, the Yukon people, who were in an ongoing war with the Shúhtaot'ine. Yamogah used his heavy wooden club to fight the grizzly bear and managed to kill it. But the bear had bitten Yamogah's thumb badly, which meant he now would have trouble holding his club and fighting other enemies. Yamogah returned to camp, knowing the bear must have been the result of a strong shaman's power and worrying about what would happen next.

Yamogah and his people were camping that night when the main attack took place. The Nahʔane sent Ayonia, a very strong warrior, to attack the Shúhtaot'ine. It was close to dawn when Ayonia the strong descended on the camp with a large group of other Nahʔane warriors. Yamogah couldn't fight back properly because of the injured thumb on his fighting hand, which by now was swollen and infected.

Too quickly all of Yamogah's people were killed, and then Ayonia came after Yamogah himself. Yamogah had a sister who at that time was living in his teepee. She yelled, "Brother!" to warn Yamogah that the Nahʔane warriors were almost upon them. "Hold onto my belt!" Yamogah yelled back at her. As she grabbed Yamogah's belt, Yamogah leapt up right through the opening at the top of the teepee, jumping clear over the enemy. The Nahʔane warriors went after them, but Yamogah was powerful with medicine and he used his power to continue straight up the side of the mountain, just as easy as if there were steps carved into it.

When he reached the mountaintop, he and his sister sat down. They watched as Ayonia and his warriors approached the base of the mountain. They taunted Yamogah, saying, "Really? Is the great Yamogah afraid of us? Come down if you aren't afraid!" Yamogah was getting mad at this taunting. He pulled out his machete knife and sliced off a whole half of the mountain. It fell forward and crushed many of Ayonia's warriors. To this day, you can still see that half of that mountain, Mackenzie Mountain, is red where it was once cut off. Yamogah yelled down at the remaining warriors, saying, "I can't defend myself properly now, but just wait until the neck of the caribou turns white. Then expect me!"

Some years passed, during which Yamogah and his sister travelled around looking for any of their people who were still alive. Once they found some of their people, but the camp was attacked the very next morning by Ayonia and his warriors and they were all slaughtered. One evening, when Yamogah and his sister were sitting outside their teepee, his sister became very sad. "Isn't there anyone alive anymore who will live with me and help us make descendants for the future?" Yamogah thought for a moment and saw that she was right. "If it's that desperate," he said to his sister, "come and walk over my legs."

His sister did so and she immediately became pregnant, which is what happens when a woman steps over someone like Yamogah with powers so strong he can make anything happen. In time she bore a son and, as the years went by, she and Yamogah raised him as a strong hunter and a warrior. The three of them kept travelling about, looking for family, but Ayonia was always one step ahead of them, killing the few Shúhtaot'ine there were. This continued for years until, finally, when Yamogah's nephew was old enough, strong enough, and well trained enough, Yamogah decided they had had enough of this suffering. It was time to get revenge against Ayonia's people, the Nahʔane, for the destruction they had caused.

Using his powers, Yamogah made all of Ayonia's people go to a place called *teh-oh-cho-wah*. This is a place in the mountains where a river flows between two peaks, a big river with sandbars all over, where people go to hunt and fish in the fall. Ayonia and all of his warriors were now gathered there to hunt and fish. Ayonia had a brother who, like him, was a very strong warrior and a good hunter. Both the brothers did a lot of hunting for their people and the people depended on them a lot.

When Yamogah, his sister, and his nephew got on top of the ridge overlooking the great river of *teh-oh-cho-wah*, they could see that there were thousands of Ayonia's people there. They watched while some of the people went hunting for sheep. One man got a sheep with his bow and arrow and pulled it to the base of the ridge, all the while staying alert in case of attack. He started butchering the sheep but stopped every now and then to look around him carefully.

Yamogah decided to take this as an opportunity. His sister and nephew kept watching as he went down the ridge and approached the man cutting up the sheep. "Ay, stranger," Yamogah said, "I'm starving. I see that you have killed a sheep. If I show you where to find some wood so you can build a fire to cook it, would you share it with me?" The stranger looked suspicious and put up his club for protection. Yamogah continued, "You see there is no wood here. If you bring the sheep down the ridge more, there you will find plenty of wood."

The man thought about it for a moment and then began to bring his sheep down the ridge. When he was at a good spot for wood he stopped. Before he could look around, Yamogah hit him with a club and killed him instantly. Yamogah then cooked the sheep and brought it back to his sister and nephew, and they feasted all night until they were very full.

The sheep was good despite the fact that Yamogah wasn't a very good cook. After they were done eating, Yamogah asked his sister and nephew if either of them would want to be the cook in future. Yamogah's sister said, "I will be the cook," so from then on, instead of fighting as a warrior, she was the cook for the group.

It was at the very same time that this was happening to Yamogah that Ayonia and his brother were hunting, too, and they had gotten a sheep. Ayonia's brother packed it and started on his way back to the camp. Yamogah's nephew saw Ayonia's brother coming right toward them and so he told Yamogah. Using his medicine powers, Yamogah took a feather from his head and blew it toward the man who was approaching them. The man turned abruptly in another direction and passed by without noticing Yamogah's group. Just in case, Yamogah also used his powers to stop the brother from seeing them. He was completely unaware that they were near.

Then Yamogah took his bow and pushed Ayonia's brother to the side. The brother fell over and got up quickly, looking around for the cause, but he saw nothing. He continued on to the main camp. Yamogah thought about how he should attack the brother and get rid of him for good. But he couldn't do that when he was invisible and the brother didn't even know he was around, it wouldn't be fair. So he put a stop to his invisibility powers and asked his nephew to cover him instead in some *t'su ele*, spruce boughs, to make him look as big as a *sahcho*, a grizzly bear. Then he would gallop off the side of a cliff. That would draw the attention of Ayonia and his warriors, who were always alert for signs of Yamogah's revenge because it was the time when the great caribou's mane begins to turn white. "Just wait until the neck of the caribou turns white," Yamogah had told them. "Then expect me!"

So, from the top of the mountain, Yamogah continued to spy on the Nahʔane, Ayonia's people, preparing to make war on them at the right time. He made sure Ayonia would not be there when he attacked by using his medicine to send him off on a hunting trip in the mountains.

When evening came, Yamogah saw some bachelors, the young people, heading to a smaller camp a little way ahead of the main camp, where the fathers, mothers, Elders, and kids were left behind. Yamogah said to his nephew, "We will attack early in the morning. The time has come!"

Early the next morning, before daylight broke, Yamogah and his nephew sat in wait to attack the two camps. They saw that two of the men were acting as lookouts from a platform on top of a tree, ready to alarm the camps if they saw any danger. Yamogah took a feather out of his hair and blew it gently toward the two people on top of the tree. When it drifted down to them, they toppled over and fell asleep.

Yamogah said to his nephew, "*Bebaa*, before we attack I will shout out a few words. You will attack the bachelors at the small camp while I attack the main camp. Start out toward the small camp and prepare to attack when I shout." His nephew set out for the small camp while Yamogah headed toward the main camp. Yamogah arrived and, when he thought his nephew had reached the other camp, he yelled out, "This is the mountains! Why are you people so sleepy!" In doing so, he hit at the first teepee in his path, shearing the entire base right out and killing everybody inside. He continued on with the next teepee and the next until there wasn't a soul left in the camp.

Then he thought about his nephew and wondered how his attack was going at the bachelors' camp. He ran toward the camp and began to pass piles of dead bodies. His nephew had killed almost all of the young men. Then he saw a person running along a ridge with his nephew right behind him in pursuit—he knew it was Ayonia's brother. Yamogah went after them, anger inside him at the suffering Ayonia and his warriors had caused by killing his people.

Ayonia's brother was running straight toward a big canyon. When he reached the cliff's edge, he made a great leap to the other side. Yamogah's nephew couldn't jump like that so he had to stop short before going over the edge. Yamogah came up behind his nephew and took a great jump to the other side, landing past Ayonia's brother. Ayonia's brother pulled up when he saw Yamogah in his path. He turned and jumped back to the other side of the canyon, but there was Yamogah's nephew. Yamogah followed Ayonia's brother and jumped back to the other side.

The brother turned and jumped across again, but this time Yamogah followed him so fast that he landed right in front of him with his club ready to deliver a deadly blow. Yamogah speared the brother with his club right through the stomach. Ayonia's brother squirmed on the club, still alive, as Yamogah dangled it over the edge of the cliff, taunting him. "Please," begged Ayonia's brother, "don't torture me, just kill me and be done with it!" Yamogah picked the brother up and threw him all the way across the canyon, yelling to his nephew, "*Bebaa*, do whatever you want with him!" His nephew picked up his own club and crushed Ayonia's brother with it, finally killing him.

Yamogah had wiped out all of Ayonia's people while Ayonia himself was out hunting for sheep with no idea what was happening. Then Ayonia was the only one left of the Nahʔane, doomed to roam the world all alone. This was what Yamogah wanted: revenge for what Ayonia had done to him and his people, the Shúhtaot'ine. The last thing Yamogah did before his vengeance was complete was to take Ayonia's brother's body and leave it on top of a big flat rock to be eaten by the seagulls. He also used his medicine power to make sure Ayonia would pass by the rock, see the body, and know what had happened to his people.

Many years later, when Yamogah and Ayonia met again, Ayonia told Yamogah the story of what happened next:

As I was walking back toward the camp, carrying all the sheep meat with me, I felt that something wasn't right. I thought to myself, "What has

*Yamogah done this time?" Then I saw a lot of seagulls eating something
on top of a big flat rock. When I got closer, I realized it was my brother's
body! Then I knew for sure it was your doing, Yamogah. The war had started
and ended without me.*

*I kept walking home, expecting to see survivors, but there were none.
The only living person I found was a little baby that had been hidden
under a pile of rawhide. I took him and tried to raise him, but he didn't
survive very long with me before he died. As I travelled the world, looking
for my people, I found that they had always been wiped out by Yamogah
before I arrived.*

*You made me suffer, Yamogah, as much as you had suffered when
I killed your people. Years and years went by, but I couldn't find a single
soul alive.*

It was true that Yamogah had travelled the world after that, always
ahead of Ayonia, wiping out every settlement of his people.

Once Yamogah came into a Nahʔane camp and attacked it, but
some of the warriors escaped by running up a high ridge. Yamogah
let out a mighty shout and turned all the warriors to stone. You can
still see that ridge today with the stones standing up on it. It's called
ʔEyǫnę náréhya, the standings of Ayonia's warriors. Another place with
similar rocks that were created by Yamogah's shouting is Kwenáréhya,
which means where the rocks are standing, a place near the mouth of
Blackwater Lake.

After that meeting between Yamogah and Ayonia, they met once
more when they were very old. This was at the same place the great war
happened, when Yamogah first killed so many of Ayonia's people. The
two powerful warriors attacked one another, but their powers were so
well matched that it was impossible for one to get an advantage over
the other. They tried and tried, but they couldn't kill one another.

So they rested and made fire and talked about the old times when
they were young and used to kill each other's people. Then, once they

got good and angry, they would start fighting again. But nothing came of it, so they rested and talked and slept.

Years went by like this, sleeping across from one another and telling each other stories by the fire. The final challenge came when Yamogah said to Ayonia, "This is the club I used to kill so many of your people. Why don't you just kill me with it!" With that, he threw his club to Ayonia. Ayonia attacked Yamogah with the powerful weapon, but still he could not kill him.

They went back to sleep by the fire and this time that is where they stayed. They slept on and on until they turned into part of the earth. To this day, on Mackenzie Mountain, across from Tulita, you can still see two great mounds across from each other with a big burnt crater between them. Some say that, when the end of time is near, Yamogah and Ayonia will wake up again.

II Oral Histories from the Life of Johnny Neyelle

Life with My Parents, Jacque Neyelle and Marie Kotoyeneh

THIS STORY is from the time of my dad and my mom.

I remember travelling all over the place with them, going wherever there was plenty of fish and wildlife. I was born in 1915 and in 1923 my parents sent us to residential school in Fort Providence, one that was run by the Catholic Church. It was during those years that I really didn't know the ways of life on the land.

In 1927, I was sent back to Fort Wrigley to stay with my parents for good. My mom Marie and my dad Jacque had asked the bishop to send us back home in consideration of their grief over losing their other son, Michel. It was after that time, back on the land, that my parents started really teaching me on-the-land skills.

My parents lived around *to-ka-toeh*, Blackwater Lake, most of their lives. Once in a while they would go into the Mackenzie Mountains to hunt mountain sheep and build moose-skin boats, and then they would come back to the community. I have five brothers and no sisters.

I went hunting a lot of times with my dad. I started at a very early age, so young that I remember my dad could pack me up and carry me when I got too tired. He showed me how to butcher moose, caribou, sheep, and beaver, how to make snowshoes, how to make fire in winter, and many other skills. He taught me about hunting moose by thinking like the moose and getting to know its habits. He also taught me how to recognize from moose tracks what kind of animal the moose was: old or young, bull or cow, and which direction it was going.

My mom taught me how to tan hide, how to sew, how to weave, and all the other basic skills of bush life, even including being a midwife. I guess that was because we were all boys in my family, with no sister to make our equipment or do other women's work.

Eventually, I guess they knew that we could all survive on our own. That's when my mom stood up and gave us a talk. She said, "You can't live with us the rest of your lives, and you can't live alone like that either. God willing, you will go and get a wife now who can take care of you." Then she added, "I myself am getting old and tired of doing all the work for you boys!"

My older brother Albert found a wife and got married in the year 1928 and moved away to raise a family of his own. We would meet him every once in a while when he came to visit Tulita (Fort Norman) to trade furs and meat to the Hudson Bay store, and we knew it would be our turn next to get wives of our own.

We were wintering around Blackwater Lake, but when summer came my parents went to Wrigley. My brother Boniface and I went to Tulita on our own. I had my own tent, boat, and dog team, everything that was needed to live off the land at that time. It was in 1941 that I decided I wanted to get married.

My mom and dad were both pleased with the woman I chose to be my wife. Her name was Rosie Yukon. We got married on July 9th of that year. My parents knew Rosie would be a perfect wife to take care of me and fulfill my needs and to take care of the children we would have. We lost five of the children we had to tuberculosis, and Rosie got it too. At that time it was really hard to cure. We were married for seven years and Rosie died on July 9th, 1948. My son Charlie was the only surviving child from our marriage.

Skeleton of a full-sized moosehide boat on the shores of the Mackenzie River. The frame is made of spruce and birch, chopped by axe and then shaped by hand with knives. The biggest moosehide boat Johnny Neyelle made took sixteen moosehides.

Both of my parents also died just before that time, and I didn't get a chance to say goodbye to them because Rosie was sick. They both passed away without me seeing them again. I had heard my mother was sick, so Rosie and I tried our best to get to her by dog team from Tulita, but she died just before we got there, the same morning. She's buried at the mouth of Dewadé, Celine River, near the banks of the Mackenzie River.

Fred Andrews was the one who told me my father was sick. It was around springtime when he told me my father was really sick at Blackwater River. I wanted to go and see him and hitched up my dog team, but there was a lot of water everywhere. I went as far as Begáhdé, where the ice had broken through. I couldn't get across and I had to turn back. It was a very painful thing to do. At the end of that month I heard that my father had died.

The summer before he died, my dad was in Wrigley. He knew it was almost his time to go, and he asked Cecilia Tally to pass on the message to me when he died. He knew I wouldn't be there when he died, so that's why he told her to tell me about it. So, early the next summer when my dad died and we were in Wrigley, Cecilia gave this important message to me. It made me think about death and life a little more. I remembered a saying that if you keep making people happy in life, you will be given more and more days to live until you get very old.

After losing my wife to tuberculosis I was single for two years. It was hard to forget the past, but life can't go on like that. You need somebody to take care of you, somebody that will make you forget the past. That's what the Elders were telling me.

So, in 1950, I got married to Joe Kenny's daughter, Jane. I asked her parents for her hand in marriage and they said yes. That's how it was in those days: if a woman had parents living, they would be the ones to decide if it was okay for her to marry you. It wasn't a decision you made on your own. Our marriage was performed by a bishop who was there in Tulita at the time. Then we moved from Tulita to Déline (Fort Franklin).

When we got to Déline, there were a lot of Elders there. I heard them talking about me, saying good things like "That person Johnny is one who really listened to his parents." The Elders of Déline knew that about me just from watching the way I hunted and worked. I had spent most of my time on the land, hunting and trapping mostly by myself all my life.

Now, today, it's the 1990s already. I don't know how many years the Lord has given me, and how many of them I have left, only the Creator knows. But I still say *máhci* to my dad for teaching me the ways of life, because to this day I'm still using that knowledge and I can't let it go.

From those years on in Déline I would travel around with my dog team, often trapping with my father-in-law Joe Kenny. I was a good hunter, so I would shoot a moose here and there while we were trapping and my father-in-law really respected me for that. The Lord gifted me with all these skills that let me live off the land and help my people with food.

My dad always used to say, "When you're among a different tribe of people, be careful how you work and hunt. So you aren't shamed by the people, try to always come home with something small, like ptarmigan or rabbit, or even something big, a caribou or a moose. Always hunt for your people, and they will be thankful for you in their hearts, even if they don't tell you." That's part of the difference between hunting and trapping. A person who is a great trapper and gets lots of furs is fine, but he only does it for himself and his family. Hunting can be used more for the people than for yourself. That's what my dad taught me when we were growing up on the land around *to-ka-toeh*, Blackwater Lake.

I went out on the land a lot trapping with my in-laws, Joe Kenny, his son Napoleon, Andrew John Kenny, and George Kenny. They got to see how I worked and hunted. Through them, lots of people learned about my life on the land. Lots of the Elders I had known since I moved to Déline in 1950 were still alive then—old Gouleo, old Sewi, Albert Menacho, and lots of other Elders.

One day, just before trapping season started, *betsée* Gouleo came to visit me. He said to me, "My nephew, I don't know how exactly to ask this, but you are a great moose hunter, so I'm asking you a favour. If you get a moose on one of your hunts this trapping season, please bring back a piece of *denek'á*, moose throat, for me."

I kept that in mind when I went out that season, and when I shot a young moose I kept the throat and also the tongue for *betsée* Gouleo. I presented them to him when I got back from the trapline. *Betsée* Gouleo said, "*Máhci, máhci*, thank you so much. You have done what I asked you to do." And he started eating the moose tongue.

Later that year, around February, *betsée* Gouleo came to see me again. He said, "My nephew, you are the only one I can think of who can carry out my wishes and make them come true. I'm asking you again for a favour. If you get another moose, and it happens to be a cow moose, please bring back the unborn calf for me to eat."

I went hunting next sometime in March. It was getting warmer and the days were getting longer. I found a moose track that belonged to a cow moose and I followed it, thinking this might be my chance to fulfill *betsée* Gouleo's request. I shot it, skinned it, and, sure enough, it had an unborn calf in its stomach. I took the calf out and brought it home with me. The next day, I boiled it and presented it to *betsée* Gouleo. He thanked me so much for it. That was the last wish he asked me to grant before he passed away in May.

I had survived on the land mostly alone all these years, but I never got tired of it. The land was my life and it gave me everything I needed. Most of the time, when I got a moose or caribou, I would think about it with gratitude. I would sit down beside it, get out my knife, and think, "My God, thank you for this fresh meat you have given me. If anyone who eats this meat doesn't pray on it, please accept my thanks on their behalf." That's how I would think the whole time I was skinning the moose. I was thanking God for it, thanking God, *máhci, máhci.*

A long time ago, our Elders were the greatest teachers we had. Think of rolling together all the professional experts, like lawyers, doctors, teachers, priests, scientists, whatever, all rolled into one—that's what they were. If you had a problem, they were the ones to ask for help.

When a person died, the Elders would tell you what to do and how to treat yourself during the time of the burial. They would help you through this time of Ets'ıhch'e, the transformation from a boy to a man that happens when you experience death. They would give you advice about how you should be very open and honest with yourself during this time.

When I was a young man, I watched William Horassi's oldest son die. He was with us in the bush when we were living off the land, and he got very sick and died suddenly. There were three families living together then, my dad's family, my brother Albert's family, and William Horassi's family.

My mother asked me to help the Horassis bury their son. She and my dad told me, "Be very careful how you handle yourself while preparing the body for burial and while burying it. Ets'ıhch'e can be very powerful. Be careful to follow the instructions given to you by the Elders." This was my first experience burying a body, so my mother tied two caribou thongs to my wrists and another two to my ankles. She said, "These will help you go through Ets'ıhch'e without any problems. Don't take them off, just let them fall off by themselves."

Other people, including Elders, gave me other advice for getting through Ets'ıhch'e. I stayed by myself. During this time, you're not supposed to sleep comfortably, so I tried using wood as a pillow. I only had a thin jacket for warmth and I would go chop wood whenever I got cold, always moving to keep from falling asleep. I always went out to chop wood before dawn, and made sure that each tent had at least four sticks.

It was over three months that I stayed like this, hardly sleeping. I also hardly drank any water, and I didn't eat any hot meals. The Elders said that if you eat a hot meal during this time, your teeth will fall out early, and if you drink water then you will always be thirsty for the rest of your life. They were following the rules of Ets'ıhch'e, and they were the ones who would usually feed you and give you some broth of rabbit or moose meat. I wore the thongs my mom tied to my wrists and ankles until they fell off by themselves.

Today, I'm still using the power of Ets'ıhch'e, so even though I only sleep a few hours, it refreshes me as if I slept eight hours. I can walk or run all day with snowshoes and never get thirsty or tired. My Ets'ıhch'e has kept me strong all my life.

If you are out hunting and cooking a meal for yourself, always leave a willow stick in front of you. If you're roasting a moose, push the willow stick inside the moose head first. Otherwise your teeth will spoil early, as soon as you get old. If you kill a moose during the time of Ets'ıhch'e, you have to disconnect or cut all the joints, every single joint you can find. You also have to talk wisely and truthfully, because if you don't, misadventure will befall you.

When you're out hunting and you want a moose or a caribou, you should ask the spirits of the animal to approach you and then it will happen. If you're checking net and taking out some fish, always take the fish head out first in the direction it's already facing. If you take the fish out tail first, you're telling the fish spirit you don't want any more fish, so always be careful how you work. These are some of the things I learned during Ets'ıhch'e. They were useful to me throughout my lifetime and still useful to me today.

I have known a lot of Elders in my lifetime, including Paul Macaulley's mom and dad; Edward Blondin, who they called *betsée* Edwaho, and his wife Kaatli; and Fred Andrew's parents and his maternal grandmother, who was called Ka-cho-reh. She died near Drum Lake and I watched four young men go through Ets'ıhch'e.

I lost my younger brother Michel when I was at residential school in Fort Providence in 1923. My mom really wanted me back home with her after that, so my parents asked the bishop and he agreed that I could be sent back to my parents, who were living in Wrigley at that time. It was fall when the steamboat *The Distributor* made its last trip up the Mackenzie River and that was the boat we jumped on. There was me, Alexie Dowyah, and Victor Lafferty's son Leon.

The steamboat stopped at Wrigley and I got off. I was supposed to meet my parents there, but they had gone hunting up the Mackenzie River. I didn't know who to stay with, but Yah-leh, David Yellee's dad, told me I could stay with them until my parents returned. About a week later, my parents came back. They had taken their time because they had shot a moose and made drymeat, pemmican, and tanned the moosehide.

After that I lived off the land with my parents. My dad used to take every opportunity to teach me about hunting. He would always let me shoot at ducks, grouse, and small game, like he was training me, I guess.

Whenever my dad shot a moose we would make camp. We would stay there until all the meat was smoke-dried, the moosehide was tanned, and every part of the moose was used for something. Nothing went to waste.

We always travelled in the bush, hunting, making camp, and moving to different places at different seasons. That was our way of life. We would go out to the bush around August and come back at Christmas. Most of the time the priest wasn't there to do Mass, but sometimes he would arrive in the summer and stay the year round, and then we would have Mass with him at Christmas.

The New Year celebrations were also a great time to renew our friendships with people we had not seen for a long time. We would go back in the bush after the New Year, so those two days were the only time we could celebrate.

When spring came around, and the ice river moved, we would go over to Tulita to sell our furs and buy groceries for the coming winter. My dad was often hired as a hunter for the Hudson Bay Company. So we would bring in a lot of moose, drymeat, dryfish, pemmican, and a lot of bone grease to trade for groceries at the Hudson Bay store.

My dad taught me really well how to stalk and hunt moose. He taught me everything you need to know about the moose itself, and even made me think like a moose, so when I hunt I know exactly what the moose is thinking about. The first moose I shot was with an Elder named Vital from Wrigley. He asked me to go hunting with him, and we went out together the next day. It wasn't long before we came upon three fresh moose tracks.

It was rutting season, so the moose were going all over the place looking for mates. We followed the tracks and stalked one of the moose. When we got close, I took my shot and watched it fall. We went over to it and, sure enough, it was dead. Elder Vital was smiling a big smile at me for shooting my first moose.

Fishing was very important to us too. When fish became scarce in one place, we would move to a different location or even another lake to get fish. When we couldn't get enough fish, we would hunt harder, looking for anything good to eat. Rabbit, ptarmigan, grouse, bears sleeping in their dens—when you're starving anything is good to eat.

When I had learned a lot about hunting, I decided to try going out to hunt alone. I had no rifle of my own, so I borrowed my brother Boniface's. I went out hunting the next day. The weather was pretty warm and the days had started getting longer too. I spotted a moose track and started following it. Since it was my first hunt alone, I wasn't really careful and quiet enough. The moose heard me and ran away before I could spot it.

I followed it for quite a ways until I saw another moose just standing by. I took a shot at that one and when I saw it fall I began to run toward it really fast. Since it was my first moose, I was a little bit scared of it. I took a long stick and poked at it to see if it was really dead. It was. That was the first moose I shot on my own. I was seventeen years old.

I have always loved hunting, and my parents loved me for that. In the springtime, around May, my dad and I would go hunting for beaver and muskrat. He would show me how to skin and clean the animals and show off his skill at cooking wild meat. He showed me how to roast a whole moose head on an open fire. There's no way you can do that kind of thing unless you are taught how.

My mother's teachings were also useful to me and impressed my dad. The first time I made snowshoes out of pine trees, my dad really liked it. He said to me, "My son, you've done a good job." I weaved the snowshoes with babiche made out of caribou hide. That weaving skill was taught to me by my mother.

Our parents always taught us well. They told us to look on the good side of life and to accept what has to happen. My brother Boniface taught me a lot as well. We went hunting a lot together and he would show me how to do certain things I didn't know about yet. He worked very well in the bush, like a professional. My dad always said, "Boniface makes a good fire—a fire worth warming up to." Even a total stranger can teach you something, if he has good wise teachings. You can learn from anyone if you listen well.

The older Elders can foresee how a person's life will be just by watching him among his people. They can see whether his life will be long or short. I guess my dad knew about Boniface's lifespan just by watching him work. He said Boniface would outlive all his five brothers and die at the age of ninety-eight, which he did.

ONE DAY *ITÁ*, my father, told me about a very good area by the mountain ridge where we could catch martin. "Why don't you pack whatever traps we have and come with me," he said, "and we'll set some traps." I packed about ten leghold traps, put on my snowshoes and the rest of my clothing, and we started walking.

When we got to the area there were a lot of martin tracks. We started setting traps. It was a very thick bush, with shrubs, willows, and trees. We got into the valley of a mountain ridge and when we ran out of traps we made fire and used some spruce boughs to build a nice place to sleep for the night.

I was wondering if we would check our traps tomorrow on our way back. But the next day my dad took another route. He said, "This is a good place for moose, this way." So, instead of checking our traps, we went back that different way. We saw a moose from the ridge, and Dad said quietly to me, "Go behind it and make sure it doesn't hear you or see you. Once you know you're behind it, make a lot of noise so when it runs it will come to me."

I started walking with my snowshoes, trying to get behind the moose without it seeing me. When I finally got around the moose, I started making a lot of noise—yelling, stomping, breaking shrubs and willows. But the moose was smart and took another route to run away instead of going to my father. So the moose escaped from us that time.

We started walking back. There was a lot of snow, so we were going very slowly. We approached a nice wooded hilly area. *Itá* broke off a piece of a long stick and went over to a big tree. He said, "There was a bear den here. I wonder if it's hibernating here again." He removed the snow from the entrance of the bear den and poked the long stick into the den until he felt something at the end of the stick. Then he let go of it. We could see the long stick moving as if by itself, and *itá* said, "Yes, there's a bear in there."

He took the stick out again and measured the top of the den. Then he told me to chop a hole through the top of it. Once I got a hole open at the top, I started poking at the bear, but it wouldn't budge. So we packed the hole with dried brushes right up to the entrance—and then we lit it on fire. A little while later, we could hear the bear grunting inside. The bear woke up and started trying to come out once the den got really smoky. As soon as the bear's head came all the way out, *itá* shot it with his muzzle-loader and it fell down. In order to pull the bear all the way out of the hole, my dad cut a hole in its lip and put a piece of willow through it. Then we pulled on the stick to pull the bear out. It was a very big black bear.

I made fire while *itá* skinned the bear. It was sometime in February, but it wasn't too cold. I made a good fire and made some tea while Dad cut out the ribs of the bear and set them by the fire to cook. It was a very fat bear, I could see from the way he had cut it. He set the rest of the bear meat on the top of the snow. When the bear ribs were cooked, we started eating it. It was delicious!

We ate and ate until we were really full. Then we put the rest of the bear meat inside the bear hide that Dad had set aside. We covered it with snow and started heading back to camp. When we got there, *itá*

Johnny Neyelle with a miniature moosehide canoe, circa 1985. Moosehide canoes were one-time-use boats used by the mountain people to get back to the trading post in Tulita in springtime when the water runs. The miniature canoe is a handicraft intended for selling.

asked my older brother Boniface to go back and pick up the bear meat with the dog team, which he did.

We had always travelled really well on land, especially in the mountains. We travelled a lot in the area around Kwechádé river and the place called *gó#erécho*, which is very good moose country and a good place to live. Another time we spent the winter at Tets'chxe, Drum Lake, and the next summer we went to visit Tulita, Fort Norman, while *itá* stayed behind at Tets'chxe. Uncle Macaulley, Dawee-ah, and Arthur's mom were also in Drum Lake at that time.

When we left Drum Lake to go to Tulita, we overnighted at a place called *eseh-gokwi*. Everything was quiet one day when we suddenly heard a gunshot. Fred Andrew was with us at that time, and he said that somebody better shoot back so whoever shot the gun would know we were there. So we shot back, and they shot back again. That's when Fred Andrew said there must be *xáhtǫnę*, strangers from another place, around. Maybe it was people who had left raw moosehide at *e-tseh-toh* to make moose-skin boats with in the spring.

It turned out that the people who were shooting were Nahʔane, Suzeh and his people who had travelled there by moose-skin boat. They knew the area well, and when they saw other raw moose skins left there they knew we were nearby. We started packing up and we took off in the direction of the shots to meet with the strangers from Nahʔane. We didn't even sleep; we just travelled all night.

Fred Andrew said at one point that somebody better go back to Drum Lake and tell the people there about the good news that we were going to meet our visitors. So it was me and Beyonnie who walked all the way back to Drum Lake to tell everyone the good news about the visitors. When we got close to Drum Lake, Beyonnie fired a shot in the air, and when we were closer to the camp he started yelling, "Pack up! People from Nahʔane came over the mountains to visit us!"

Without sleeping, everyone packed up their belongings and then all of us, including the Elders, started back on the way to where the visitors were. We overnighted at *eseh-gokwi* again, and the next day we got to where the rest of our people and the visitors were meeting. Oh boy, were they ever so happy to see each other! It was a time of joyful reunion. For the whole week at least we stayed there together.

We made two very large moose-skin boats, about thirty feet long each. Once we finished making the boats, we all left together. I didn't ride in the moose-skin boat but instead in a smaller canvas boat with an outboard motor. Tłdedele daetłʼı was where we were heading the next day. When we passed that place, the strangers started shooting into the water, saying that was how they were paying respect to the land. We came upon a moose on one of the islands, and they shot it. From that point it wasn't too far to the Dehcho, the Mackenzie River.

Suzeh, Tse-tsah, and Bean, those three families together had made a huge moose-skin boat that carried all of their gear, their dogs, the wives and kids—food, tent, stove, sled, dog harnesses, everything they owned was in the boat. Finally, we got to Dehcho and it got quieter there because the river is so smooth. We reached Tulita, Fort Norman, a day later and there were a lot of people there to greet us on the shore. We stayed in Tulita all that summer, June, July, and August. Then we all went back to Drum Lake.

Paul Macaulley and I went back on our own, in our little outboard motor. We went up Begáhdé and got back to *e-tseh-toh*. From there we went overland with our dog packs to Drum Lake. When we got there, the people that had already gotten back before us had just left again. We heard a shot up ahead of us, announcing where they were, so we answered with our own shot and they answered back with another. We decided to catch up with them and walked along the shore until we reached their new camp.

While they were in Drum Lake these people had made a whole bundle of dryfish, which they were enjoying now. My mom had made ten bundles of dried fish, which was a lot. In Drum Lake, Paul Macaulley's father had shot seven moose, so there was a lot of drymeat too. There was lots of fresh meat and fresh fish as well, but everyone was running out of tea, sugar, and flour. After a couple of days we moved again. We really enjoyed living off the land—it was our whole life.

Later on, the visitors from Nahʔane came back to us again. They used a trail across from Fort Norman and went overland past Begáyué, over Néréla, and finally to Tets'chxe, Drum Lake. Some of the visitors stayed at Drum Lake and some others went to another area for the winter.

We decided to go into the mountains ourselves. We stored our sled, harnesses, and a few groceries in a log cabin we had built and, with only our guns and our dogs carrying packs, we moved inland. On our way to the mountains we shot moose, caribou, and bighorn sheep, so there was a lot of work to do just to dry all the meat.

We finally got to the end of the barrens in the mountains. Once all the meat was dried, we went up to the river where we made a huge cache, all bundled up in rawhide and tied to a long wooden pole tied in to the very top of a big tree. We took a look at the moosehides we had and they looked good enough for a moose-skin boat, so we decided to build one. After we had built our boat, we continued on our way by water.

There was a group that had split off from us on the way from Drum Lake and continued on to Tútsituwé. Wilson Pelissey's mom was with that group, and Wilson was still travelling with us. When we got to a place where Suzeh had wintered before, we saw a *daht'o*, a big platform, which they had made way at the top of a tree to store all their gear. Suzeh got out of the boat and went to check if all of the things they had left were still there. We followed behind him.

Then Suzeh noticed a letter that someone had written and nailed to a tree. He picked up the note and looked at it. It was written in Dene syllabics. I took the note and started reading it and I saw it was a bad news letter. It said that Wilson Pelissey's mother, who was at a fish lake with some other people, had died.

Wilson was still in the boat, but he got out and started walking up to us as we were reading the news. Suzeh, being the eldest, told him what happened. "My nephew," he said, "your mom died. There's no use saying anything about it now, so be strong and don't say anything."

The Elders talked to Wilson, helping him be strong by telling him about the way life is and how you have to let go. Suzeh and his people collected all the winter gear from their platform and loaded it into the moose-skin boat, and then we left. The other group was now camping at a fork in the river called Tuts'ınlı, which was where they were waiting for us. From there, we would go down the river and then get out and go overland, by Néréla, to Tets'chxe, Drum Lake. Some other people went to Fort Norman, but we continued overland to Tets'chxe.

We had a lot of dried meat and gear, so the going was slow and the dogs were tired. We decided to camp for the night and, as we had no tea or sugar, I went ahead to see if I could pick up some tea at a cabin where we had stored some and bring it back to the people. I was alone and travelling as fast as I could. When I got to the cabin, I found some tea and some sugar and turned right back. On the way back, I was travelling along the river when I spotted the people I had left, who were now moving along again in my direction.

I located some good packed ground and made a fire and a big pot of tea. One by one, my group started arriving until finally everyone was there. We had a big tea party with sugar and smoked some cigarettes. Boy, tea sure tastes good when you haven't tasted it for a long time! We camped there that night and left the next morning, and finally got back to Drum Lake. Yahtsuleh, Fred Andrew's dad, was also with us then.

Here, Johnny recounts a story in the voice of his father, Jacque.

AT THE TIME OF THIS STORY, we were moving around a lot. There was hardly any rabbit around to snare for food. We had just moved to a place we thought might be good for rabbit. A couple of families moved on a little farther up the river to see if there was any rabbit there. This was all happening in the Blackwater Lake area.

With no rabbit, no spruce grouse, nothing, there was hardly any food for our family to eat, and we were starving. My older brother Xah-chile hunted a lot, but he didn't bring back anything. It was the same with my brother Ma-zee. I was still young and I didn't have a wife yet. My grandmother was with us then. She used to kind of sleep on my feet, using them as a pillow. That's why it seems like my grandmother was the one who raised me.

One night it was getting really cold, but I still went out to check the rabbit snares. There were two trails to check with lots of snares on each one, but still I had caught nothing. Once in a while we were getting one or two rabbits, but that wasn't near enough. Back then there wasn't any whiteman food. It was all land food.

I went out soon after that first time to check the snares again, but there was still nothing. It was getting tougher and tougher. When I got back home, my mom gave me the two small front feet of a rabbit, with sinews attached. That was all she had for me to eat. I was very hungry, but I gave the rabbit paws to my youngest brother Eli.

I told my family I was going hunting, and I took off. I started walking in my snowshoes to an area that I thought might have big game around. I didn't know whether I would make it back or not, but if we didn't eat, none of us would make it, so I went.

I didn't see any grouse or ptarmigan during that whole long walk in my snowshoes, but I kept going. As I reached a dry wooded area, I spotted a moose running toward the dense willow trees on the other side. I wasn't at all prepared to spot a moose, since I hadn't seen any moose tracks, so I didn't have my muzzle-loader ready. The moose disappeared into the thick willows and I lost it.

I was so angry with myself. I thought, "I was hoping to get a moose—that's why I came here. How did I let this happen?" I stood there for a long time, thinking about what had happened. Then I continued on. I thought to myself, "I've come this far. I'm not backing off now!"

I kept on walking, looking for grouse or anything else that might come my way, and keeping my eye out now for moose tracks too. I didn't see any moose tracks, but as I entered a clear area with smaller trees I spotted a dotted object across the muskeg that looked to me like two spruce grouse sitting on a snowbank. I wondered what it really was—although it looked like two grouse, it was moving sideways and then back to the same position in a strange way. "It can't be grouse, then," I thought—"It's a moose!"

I took off my snowshoes and started pushing through the deep snow. It was really thick. I kept pushing myself through it, closer and closer to the moose I had spotted, with my muzzle-loader loaded and ready. The moose was sleeping in some brush, deep in the snow with its ears sticking out. I got close enough to shoot it and stopped there.

From where I was, I couldn't see the moose's whole body. I broke off
a piece of a twig and the moose turned its head in my direction. It
listened for about five minutes, then turned its head back again. I knew
that if I broke another twig the moose would bolt. I got my muzzle-
loader ready and broke another twig. The moose got up, startled, and he
was sideways to me, which gave me a good shot. I knew I only had one
shot to make before the moose bolted, so I aimed steady and pulled the
trigger. I didn't even know if it would shoot properly because of the cold
weather.

But it did. The moose jumped when I shot at it and stumbled into
the thick willows. The sounds I heard told me I had hit it. I went back
to get my snowshoes and packsack and then returned to the spot
where I had shot the moose. I found traces of moose hair and blood on
the snow and I was sure I had got it. I followed that trail just a little
way before I found the moose dead in its tracks.

I made fire right away and prepared to skin the moose. It was a
cow moose, a very good moose for eating, that I had shot. I skinned the
moose and then I wanted to eat it right away. But I didn't eat it for a
long time. I decided to just make some broth first. Elders always say
you should never start with anything solid if you haven't eaten for a
long time.

It had gotten dark while I was skinning the moose, and as I started
walking toward where I wanted to make camp, I used the stars and
the treetops as guides. I found my own tracks again and followed them
until it was very late at night. Then I saw some traces of smoke coming
out of the teepees at the camp up ahead of me.

I got right to the entrance of the teepee and took my snowshoes off,
but then I thought it would be good to also bring something else. I was
having good luck now finding something to eat, so I went back outside
and right away I shot a *dih*, a spruce grouse. By then it was really
dark. I returned to the teepee and I could hear my mother speaking
inside. I walked in with my load of fresh meat and everyone was there,
including my grandmother who was still alive then. We shared the

moose meat with our neighbours, my brother Ma-zee and his family, who only drank the broth.

There were also some other families living by the rivers a few miles away from us, like Ne-keh-ya *betá*'s and Vidal's families, who had been starving that winter. The next morning, two young men packed up some of our meat and went to visit those families and share it with them. They were very grateful, and they asked if a couple of their young men could come back to our camp and pack up some more of the meat to bring back.

Ne-keh-ya *betá* couldn't go because he had a heart problem, so Vidal *betá* and one of the younger men came along to get some more meat. They trekked right by our camp to where the moose meat was and packed it up. By the time they got back home, it was really dark because the days were short then. Two other meat packers from another camp spent the night with us and then left early in the morning with their load of meat for their people.

As they were walking home, they later told us, they spotted something odd on the snowshoe trail. Once they got closer, they saw that it was a person, frozen solid. It was Ne-keh-ya *betá*. I guess he followed them in spite of his heart condition. He must have blacked out and then he froze to death. The young men brought the bad news back to both camps right away. That must have been why I couldn't get a good chance to shoot the moose when I first saw it on the trail—because death was around, waiting to strike. But I still shot the moose in the end.

After I shot that moose, and shared the meat with everyone, it was like a curse had been lifted. Everything went back to normal: we started catching rabbits in our snares, hunters got more moose and caribou, and it seemed that the starvation period was finally over. I had broken whatever curse had been put on our tribe. After Ne-keh-ya *betá* died, his widow married Ma-zee. That's what life was like in the early 1700s. And that was the first time I used my powers to help my people, the Shúhtaot'ine.

Another time, we were moving around the mountain area where there was lots of big game. We decided to go back to Dehcho, the Mackenzie River, and we started moving. Ahead of us, our two hunters Ma-zee and Xah-chile were making trail. Xah-chile was packing a bear hide that he had shot in the fall. Bear hide was bought by the Hudson Bay Company back then, so it was worth a lot. We hardly had anything to eat at this time, and whatever the hunters got we would all share.

Much of the time there was nothing at all to eat, so we would have to keep moving on an empty stomach for maybe two or three days. After travelling like that for several days, with little to eat and a caribou-skin sled, I decided to go up with the hunters. I put on my snowshoes and caught up to them. They had overnighted and were just preparing to leave when I reached them. They looked at me and said, "Hey brother, what are you doing here? We have nothing to eat. We even had to eat part of that bear hide we were carrying. You should stay with the rest of the family back there."

I thought there must be some big game around, and it angered me that someone must be keeping it away from us. I stood there angry for a long time, not saying anything in response. Then they were ready to leave. I thought to myself, "We can't eat bear hide. There must be some game around somewhere!" and I said to them, "You go ahead. I'll warm up a little and catch up with you." They went on ahead, and I took off in a different direction to find game.

I was certain we were going through another starvation curse. I walked along through the dense wilderness in my snowshoes. All of a sudden, a moose stood up right in front of me, out of nowhere. Without even thinking, I pulled out my muzzle-loader, aimed, and fired. The moose disappeared into the bushes. I used my only shot—with a muzzle-loader you can't load very fast, so you often only get one good shot to make.

I was reloading it when Xah-chile came out of the trees. He and Ma-zee had heard my gunshot. "What are you shooting at?" Xah-chile yelled to me. He started walking in the direction I pointed out, and soon we saw the moose dead on the ground. My brother Xah-chile looked at me and said, "My brother, how did you do this?" I didn't say anything. Then Ma-zee came toward us and when he arrived he helped us skin the moose. After skinning and cleaning the moose, we went back to the trail and made a good fire, a signal to the families who were following us. They shared in the moose meat and it helped get us through that hard period of starvation.

That was twice in my lifetime that I had gotten my people out of starvation. Even though our people have good hunters, sometimes it gets really tough.

These events reminded Johnny of another story his dad had told him when he and his siblings were young, about his own father, Yamochile, who helped his people through starvation. When that story was over, Johnny's mother turned to the kids and said, "I wonder if you boys, my sons, will ever do something like that."

So this story is also the story of Morris's great-grandfather, Yamochile, descendant of the mountain people, the Shúhtaot'ine.

A Trip to Mackenzie Mountain

WE MOVED TO TULITA, Fort Norman, around 1930, and went into the Mackenzie Mountains twice. Both my parents were still living at that time. It was a long and treacherous trip into the mountains, and we had to use our dog packs for the journey.

Close to the mountains, at their edge, there's a fish lake called Kwetenıa. That was our usual stopping place where we would set net and make dryfish for our trip. We usually had hunters going ahead of us at all times, and when they shot a moose or caribou that's where we would make camp for the night and roast a moose head for the Elders.

This time, we had made camp way past Kwetenıa. There were a few families travelling together then. Beh-gah-leh's father, Yenee-toh, Tsee-tsa, and my family had split from the main group; we went toward Begáyué ridge while the others went to the treeline in the mountains.

We spent one night at the ridge and the next day we travelled again. My dad, Jacque Neyelle, and Beh-gah-leh's father, Yenee-toh, were ahead of us. They had shot a moose, but we passed them and kept on straight toward our destination and spent the night on our own. The next morning they met us there with their sacks full of meat. That was the first moose killed on the trip.

Néréla was where we headed after that, and Beh-gah-leh's father was our head guide. He was really proud of himself for that, thinking he was a big leader, which made us laugh.

At that time, Yeh-nee-toh's mother was still alive. She travelled with us using a willow cane, going at a slow pace but always staying with us. We started to slow down because we had shot another moose and our load was getting heavier.

Then it happened that A-she-gee's mom couldn't walk anymore. We were still one full day from Begáhdé, but she was paralyzed and we couldn't help her to move at all. We ended up making a big hammock and carrying her in it all the way to the Begáhdé river. We left her there with Beh-gah-leh, Dora-day, and A-she-gee to take care of her until we returned from hunting in the mountains.

We stayed a few days and then continued on our way to the mountains. We told the people we left behind that we would be gone for at least two or three weeks, sooner if the hunting was really good and later if it wasn't. With that, we made a raft and crossed the river. We had a lot of dog packs, so every river crossing was really slow going.

Gah-leh's father and my father were up ahead of us looking out for moose or caribou tracks. We were following their lead when we noticed some moose tracks leading across to an island, which they hadn't seen. I ran after them and told them about the moose tracks. Since they had gone across to an island, we should be able to hunt them down easily.

Then I started running really fast in the direction of the trail. Suddenly, right in front of me appeared a bull moose. I didn't have a gun with me so I just yelled, as loud as I could, "There's a moose standing right in front of me!" The moose was startled and bolted into the river. It started swimming toward the island where the others had already gone. Our dogs were wild with hunger at that point, and when they saw the moose fleeing the whole pack of dogs bolted in pursuit, jumping into the river, dog packs and all!

Soon the moose got across the river to the little island and we shot it. Then some of the dogs turned back, knowing they might drown under the weight of their packs if they tried to go all the way across. The strongest dog in the pack turned back too, barely making it to dry ground. When he got back, we saw it was because he was carrying all our ammunition that the swim was so difficult.

We decided to make camp there. My brother Boniface and our friend Thomas made a raft and went across the river to tow the moose back to us. We made camp while they were on their way. When they returned with the moose, we butchered it and left it on a rack to smoke dry during the night. We had so many dogs it was easy to carry the moose meat with us. Ten to fourteen dogs can carry a good-sized load of semi-dried moose meat with no problem at all.

We continued on the next day, spending a couple more nights along the river. Finally, Gah-leh's father said, "From here on, let's go to the ridge. It's good hunting there for moose." We wanted to shoot as many moose as possible because we intended to make a moose-skin boat to use on our trip back down the river. We kept the hide from every moose we shot.

After days and days of travelling and getting several moose, we started to pack all the moose meat back down to the riverbank. We made a huge raft and crossed the river, hauling the moose, caribou, and Dall sheep meat and everything else we were carrying. We made a few trips across the river to get everything across.

After that, we decided not to shoot any more sheep because it just made too much work for us to haul everything. We made a good camp after that crossing and got to work making drymeat, pemmican, and bone grease. We made a big moose-skin bag and filled it with all our dried moose meat, then tied it to a long pole that we balanced in one of the tallest trees. We put a few of those poles with bags of meat up all along the river to pick up later. Then we were only carrying with us the dried moose skins for our boat.

We were ready to go back on the river, and Gah-leh's father pointed out a good place up ahead where we could make our moose-skin boat. We made a teepee with high poles and hung the last of our meat there to dry while we were away. Gah-leh's father said, "If you don't think at all about the meat we left behind, nothing bad will happen to it, and it will definitely be there when we come back for it. So don't think about it!" And, with that, we left.

We got to the place Gah-leh's dad had pointed out and he was right, it sure was a good place to make a boat. From our camp there, we could see across the mountain ridge to a place where sheep liked to go in the early morning to find salt licks. Beh-gah-leh's father said that we could hunt the sheep there right from our moose-skin boat. We had constructed a huge frame by then, using long timbers and small trees and then twelve moose skins stretched over them, six at the bottom and three on each side, secured with sinew. It had taken us a good few days to do that.

One morning, after it was done, we saw a whole herd of sheep heading toward the salt licks. We decided to get some for our trip back. Everyone except for me got in our boat and snuck behind the ridge to surprise the sheep. I went around the other side of the ridge to wait. When the others fired their shots at the sheep, they all stampeded toward me at a full gallop. I shot some and I missed some. After the ones we had missed disappeared behind the ridge, we counted the ones we had gotten. There were twenty-three sheep altogether.

It was a lot of work to pack them up, but that kind of work was our life and we enjoyed doing it. We hauled the meat back to camp all that day, going back and forth with multiple loads until it was done.

We loaded our moose-skin boat the next day and went down the river to pick up the meat we had left behind to dry—that would have been about a week ago now. When we got back to the place where we left the meat on the teepee poles, it was all still there. Nothing had happened to it, even though there were so many bears and other animals around. I knew then that we had strong mental medicine powers not to think about the meat so it would stay safe, just as Gah-leh's father had said.

We stopped at all the places we had cached meat and loaded it into our huge moose-skin boat as we paddled down the river. We over-nighted at one of the cache sites and moved the meat around a bit so we would have more room in the boat. Early in the morning we left again and continued our trip down the river.

We shot another moose while we were travelling down the river and stopped to skin it and butcher it. Then we loaded it back into the boat and continued on. We decided not to shoot any more moose after that, unless they were really easy to get right on the shoreline.

Yah-nee-toh was the one steering the main paddle at the back of the boat, so he became kind of the boat captain. We spent another night by the river and the next day when we continued on we were starting to get pretty close to the place where we had left Gah-leh's mother behind. We took a shot in the air to let them know we were coming, and soon after we heard an answering shot from their side. We took another shot and they answered that one too.

Yah-nee-toh said, "That's enough shooting—they're doing fine." Elders know the situation other people are in by how many shots they fire: if it's one shot, that's not good news, but if it's two shots every-thing is fine.

As we were approaching the camp, we saw Gah-leh's mother, who was totally paralyzed when we left her, walking around and waving at us. That was a great sight for us to see! We soon saw that everyone else was doing fine too.

The next day, we packed up all their gear with ours, loaded everyone in the boat, and headed back toward to the great Dehcho, the Mackenzie River. We spotted three more moose along the river and shot them all, loading them into the boat and then continuing on our way toward Tulita.

When we finally got there, we shared most of our dried meat and gave our raw moosehide to the local lady to tan. We stayed there for a few days and then headed on to *to-ka-toeh*, Blackwater Lake, for our winter trapping.

This was just one of the mountain trips I did when I was growing up, and that kind of thing was my whole life.

The Dream, 1940s

THIS STORY THAT I'M SHARING NOW is the story of a dream
that was sent to me when I was really sick. In this world, when you're
not sick, you don't dream much. But when you're sick, you begin to
dream and to see things from other worlds really vividly.

I didn't know what it was that I had at first, or if I was dying or
what, I just knew that I felt really sick. I was in Déline, and since there
was no nurse or anything here, Elder Jimmy Cleary took me over to
Tulita by boat to be taken care of. It must have taken about four or five
hours to get there, but because I was so sick it seemed to me like an
hour or less.

When I got to Tulita, they put me straight in the hospital and gave
me some medication that put me to sleep right away. When I got up
the next morning, I felt like my body was cooked—it was some effect
of the medication they had given me. I felt much better than before,
though. At that time, Suzie Tutcho's son Jean was also in the hospital.

I was really weak and tired after I woke up, so I went back to
sleep pretty quickly, and that's when I had a powerful dream. I felt
myself being taken to the spirit world, the land of the departed, when

suddenly I felt a hand on my shoulder. "Wait," a voice said, "your time is not up yet. You have to turn back from here."

I realized it was my protector, my guardian who was speaking to me. I could feel him, but I couldn't see him. So I turned around and started travelling back to the real world, the world of the living. I went past the ramparts in Fort Good Hope and that's where I lost contact with the vision. Then I saw Bear River and Mackenzie River at Tulita. I turned down the Bear River route because that's the way back to where I came from.

I was on top of a cloud, looking down the mouth of Bear River at the buildings across the lake and the beautiful lake itself, and all the time my guardian was with me. I saw a circle of clouds around me, from the sunrise to the sunset, both of which were happening at once.

I saw millions upon millions of people, their heads sticking right out of the clouds. My guardian let me know that these were all the people who had died since the beginning of the world, who were still awaiting their final fate on Judgment Day.

Then my guardian told me to look at the mouth of Bear River. I looked closely and saw something strange, a big black being of some kind blocking the entrance to the river. That black shape was made of the leftover energy of bad medicine power that had been used years earlier.

"You passed by that and it touched you," my guardian told me. "That's why you got sick. But today I will get rid of that bad energy forever." He used his own powers on that big black mass and it disappeared. "From now on it will be safe to travel through here," he said.

I was thinking about all the people who had died sitting up there in the clouds. I wondered if the great prophet Louis Ayah was there too. "Yes, yes," my guardian answered me, even though I hadn't said anything out loud. He could hear my thoughts.

"Look over there," he added, "that's where your people are sitting." I turned and looked toward the sun, toward the east where it rises. I could see rows and rows of people sitting in the clouds there, and at the very end of the rows was a bright light shining.

I wondered why all these people had to sit in waiting to finally have rest after they had already left the living world. My guardian tried to explain by telling me that if people get married with sin in their hearts, they will suffer greatly when they die. So, to give these kinds of people a chance to rest peacefully, they are sent to a waiting place with everyone else, who waits with them to help take some of the sin away through sharing it.

I saw some people sitting in those clouds who had done what my guardian described: *betsée* Owen-teo who married Johnny Takazo, and also Jean Tutcho who married Cecilia Tatti. Both of them died really early—they didn't last long at all. I guess even though God loves us, we create problems for ourselves that are really hard to deal with.

Then I wondered to myself what the most important commandment was to follow while you're on Earth if you want to see the kingdom of God at the end of time. My guardian said, "Look over there," pointing toward an old man, an old woman, and a lot of young children standing around them. "These are the people who you need to help most while you're on Earth, the old people and the orphans," he said. "That pleases God the most, since those people often have nobody to help them though they need it most."

I thought again then about all those people just waiting for Judgment Day, and I wondered how we are to be judged. "Look over there," my guardian said, pointing in another direction. I looked that way, and in the clouds I saw many, many people, maybe millions, following a path. There was a fork in the path with one branch going left and one going right. Some people went one way and others went the other. "Everything you do on Earth is already known," my guardian said, "so when you get to this fork it is already known how you will be directed."

I thought about the evil called the devil and how he worked on people and what he did to them if they went his way at the fork in the path. Down one branch of the path I could just see what looked like a big steering wheel screwed over a burning flame. Suddenly, a burst of blue flame shot out from the fire with a loud, loud blast of sound. The flame was wide and long, stretching into the air for miles. That was the fire of the devil, the guardian told me.

Then the guardian told me about the way women were the first ones to commit sin, by stealing an apple from the Garden of Eden. Because of that, the guardian said, women shouldn't have important names in this world. I looked around the clouds and I saw a woman and a man both wearing crowns, like a queen and a king. The guardian said that the woman's crown was to be taken away; it would just fade away slowly over time until it vanished completely. That's the way it has to be—women can't have a leadership role in this world.

I remember Louis Ayah talking to my dad about alcohol back in the early 1930s. Ayah was talking about something called "The Book of Alcohol," or *kǫtú erıhth*. He said that there were many copies of this book laid end to end across the world, from where the sun rises to where it sets. The books were bound in covers of many colours: red, blue, green, yellow, purple.

I remembered that story when I saw the vision of the Book of Alcohol in my dream. The guardian noticed me looking at it and he made me realize something. I thought to myself that alcohol represented a part of my life that I wasn't keeping very well. I had heard a lot of negative things about alcohol in my life, yet I kept on drinking. I guess that's why I'm not feeling well today.

I realized in this dream that there is a greater power out there, and if I keep on doing bad things in my life, my life will be taken away early. I thought about how I would be like a broken stick later in life, and that's why I always pray a lot. I won't want to be like a broken stick. What does it mean to be so broken? I think to myself.

This dream that was shown to me when I was sick is something I never described to anyone in my life before now, but somehow the prophet Old Andre knew about it. One day he came to visit me and he said, "That dream you had way back when is a true vision." Somehow he knew about the dream.

Máhci, máhci.

SOMETIMES WHEN I WOULD GO HUNTING when I was young I would sit down and think for quite a while. Usually, getting one or two moose happened really easily for me when I went out hunting. I never depended on anybody—it was always me alone, always alone. That's how I was, just living in the wilderness alone.

I know some people think, "How can a person do that?" but it wasn't really me all alone. I also had God my creator and all the stories and advice my dad gave me. That's what has kept me alive until today, *máhci*.

I will tell you some stories about my father. One day, way back years ago when I was still a young man, my parents told me and my brothers that, God willing, we would live a very long life, that we would be around long after they were both gone, and that we had to accept that someday they would leave us. I always remember that story. It's still with me today, as clear as if I just heard it yesterday.

My dad taught all of his sons the survival skills we needed to live off the land and also how to live life in a good way. He taught us to listen to stories, saying, "If a young person listens very closely to a story, he will survive a long time, but if he moves about and fidgets and doesn't pay attention, his life will be shortened, just like a broken stick."

That's exactly what happened here not too long ago. Three boys drowned driving their Ski-Doos into the open water. If they had listened to their Elders more closely, that never would have happened. It was an accident the Elders could have warned them about. My mother always told me to listen to Elders, especially before I had any of my own dreams and visions. Elders have already had their visions and seen their grey hair, so they know about the future.

"Listen to what your dad is telling you," my mom would say to me. "It is like a straight path he is pointing out for you to follow that will take you through a long life. This path doesn't mean your life will be perfect—there will be tough times and problems of all kinds, some of which will be very painful. But you can use this path your dad is building for you to find a way through that."

My parents would also say that they didn't tell us stories just because they wanted to or we wanted them to, but because these stories were passed on to us from our ancestors, who had been telling these stories for thousands of years before us. They know life because they've lived it. The Bible tells us to respect your Elders, and it's the same in Dene culture. Whoever respects their Elders will live a long time.

Sometimes, when bigger problems occur, you just know that death is waiting for you. But, God willing, you can slip past it. That happened to me once. I was hunting by a river called Dewadé, Celine River. It was warm, windy, and snowing. I was walking along the river, looking for moose tracks in my hunting snowshoes, which were about six feet long and sixteen inches across at the centre. Because they were so big, I could walk on the snow easily.

When I got to the river, I wanted to cross it to look for moose on the other side. I started walking across, but when I was about halfway I thought I heard a scream. I stopped and listened, wondering who was around. Then I heard that whoever it was was calling my name.

"Johnny, Johnny..." that's what I heard. I looked around for a while, but nobody appeared, so I continued walking.

Then I heard my name called again, louder this time. I stopped to listen, and that's when I heard water flowing under the ice right in front of me. I picked up my gun and tapped the ice in front of me and the whole chunk of river ice fell, leaving my feet in my big snowshoes sticking halfway out over the edge of the ice, hanging over the open flowing water.

I was shaking, I was so scared. But I backtracked very carefully and quietly, and made it back to the mainland. It wasn't my day to die, and that's why my voice was being called as I went across the river toward death. It's because I listened to my parents that I paid attention to that voice and that's why I was saved that day.

These are the kinds of incidents that wait for you on the path of life. I call this one a miracle because I survived. If I hadn't listened to my parents, and used what they taught me, my life would have ended right there, in that river, like breaking a stick.

My dad really taught us about life. We used to have such long walks in the wilderness while we were hunting, and we would be really cold because often we had no tent, even in temperatures of minus thirty-five degrees or colder. Whenever it got cold, I would just get up and chop more wood to put on the fire. My dad liked what I was doing and liked the way I worked, so he would always teach me more.

How you work on the land, how you treat people, the way you behave— Elders can know your future just by watching these things. The Elders are like dictionaries that hold the answers to all kinds of things. It's important to carry on the knowledge that Elders and parents give us. "My children," my parents would say, "when you have a wife and kids of your own please pass on to them the knowledge that we are giving to you, so they can also use it."

In the old days, people would live by medicine powers that were given to them when they were young, which they had to earn, but those days are gone now. You still have to remember to be respectful, though, and to use your skills in the right way.

When you are hunting for moose or caribou, you are always hunting for your community, your people. If you are alone with your family, then you can keep whatever you get, but if you go out from a community, you should always try to bring back at least a ptarmigan, a grouse, or something. If you don't do that then people will talk about you and say all kinds of things, wondering what kind of hunter you are who brings nothing back to share with the people.

I'm glad to have used the land so well throughout my life. Sometimes, when I hunt alone in the fall, it's dark—pitch black. But it never even crossed my mind to be afraid. My dad used to tell us that there was a Bushman who sometimes attacked hunters in the dark, but it wasn't any good to be afraid of him. "This land is so vast," he would say. "How can the Bushman know where you are, or that you're alone? It's a very slim chance he would ever find you, so don't worry about him." Sometimes I hear other people worrying about the Bushman, and sometimes it seems justified, but most of the time it doesn't. Most of the time people worry that something drastic will happen and the spirit of someone deceased will start travelling about and bothering us—that's what most people see.

My father taught me many different skills. With water, for instance, he taught me that just because it freezes doesn't mean you can walk on it. Always carry a long pole when walking on ice, so if you fall through you can save yourself. Not all ice is the same thickness either. Ice with a lot of snow on it is thinner and so is river ice, because the current flowing under it makes it thin.

Every day and every night we would get advice like that from my parents, and to this day I live by their words and their wisdom. I'm so thankful to my parents for teaching me well.

My parents stopped teaching me things once I was old enough. It was at this time that my mom said to me, "Find someone else to sew your mukluks. I'm getting old and tired, and I won't be around much longer. You need a partner to take care of you." She was talking about getting married and starting my own family. I was worried about that, because I didn't really have anything. I thought, "How can I get married with nothing?" But it was all about earning it—if you deserve a wife, you prove it by showing how well you can survive alone.

After I got married to my first wife, Rosie Yukon, my father and mother didn't tell me any more stories. From then on, the decisions I made were mine and I was the only one who would decide how to live my life.

Only once did my mother ask me for help. Just before Christmas one year, we were staying by Dewadé, Celine River. My Uncle Macaulley and his family were staying at *to-ka-toeh*, Blackwater Lake. There was hardly any food. We couldn't snare any rabbits or grouse, and we were starving. My mother came into our tent and said, "Johnny, why don't you go hunting? You always get something. It's close to Christmas and we have nothing to eat."

I thought about what my mom had asked and I realized that she's right. She raised me since I was born and she knows me well enough to know that I could probably get a moose even when nobody else could. I didn't say anything, but the next morning I got up early and grabbed my snowshoes, gun, and packsack and disappeared into the wilderness.

I got back late that evening, and when I returned I brought with me a load of moose meat from the cow moose I had shot. My wife Rosie stuck her head out of the tent and when she saw me coming she called to my mother, "*Betsį*, a moose has been shot!" My mother came over to our tent to see what I had got. "It's a cow moose," I told her, and she was all smiles. She was so happy and also very proud of me.

My mom gave me a lot of advice when I was young, just as my dad did. She taught me how to sew mukluks, tan moosehide, weave snowshoes, and do all the other women's work that needed to be done, even including delivering babies. "What if your future wife can't do these things well?" she would sometimes say, talking to me while tanning moosehide or doing other women's work. "It'll be up to you to train her." And, saying that, she would giggle a little. She was right, though, because as of today you don't see a lot of the girls sewing or tanning hides. I saw my dad tan a beaver hide once, using different ingredients from the land. The hide came out all fluffy and perfect. I can still do it like that.

"We raised and trained you young men to take care of your family," our parents would tell us. "To go hunting when there's not enough to eat, to survive and never give up, that's your job. Women are trained to take care of the kids, and that takes up a lot of time, so sometimes they won't be able to do other things around the camp, like chop wood. So you should help out the women as well and always check when you come back from hunting to see if there's any wood. If there isn't any, go get some and then go inside."

These are important lessons that we should keep carefully and pass on.

ONE TIME, when I was younger, I wanted to go out to Whiskeyjack Point. I loaded my hunting gear, along with a tent, gas lamp, and stove and headed out on my little Ski-Doo Elan. When I had travelled a fair distance, I noticed that my Ski-Doo was kind of wobbling. I stopped and checked the Ski-Doo and saw that one of the skis was broken almost in half!

I wasn't sure what to do, but I had a lot of rope with me, so I used that to tie the ski together as tight as possible. It worked well enough to get me to the shores of Whiskeyjack Point.

I needed to set a tent then, so I did that first. Then I started chopping some wood for the stove, but all of a sudden my axe handle broke off! I had the stove ready by that point, so in order to fill it up a little I put down the broken axe and started breaking up kindling with my hands and feet. It was getting dark on me and I needed to light my gas lamp because I hadn't brought any candles. I managed to make a small fire in the stove.

Then I tried to light the gas lamp, but the generator needle inside broke off! That left me with very little light, just what was cast by the

Johnny Neyelle's hunting gear: a moose caller made out of birchbark, a Winchester .30-30 lever-action rifle bought in 1933, a knife, a file, and a bone scraper.

stove. But I needed to repair my axe handle, so I grabbed my packsack and started looking for my knife in the dark. I couldn't see it, so I kept looking and looking, but finally I realized I must have forgotten it.

I only had a small pocket knife. I had to make do with that and began to try to make an axe handle using that little pocket knife. It took a while! I had to stop because there was so little light, and I started fiddling around with my gas lamp to get it working again. Finally, I got it to light up, but it was a very dim light. At least it was a little better than before, and in my dim light with my little pocket knife I was able to fashion a very rough axe handle.

Then I gathered some wood and chopped it to a good length so I could stay warm during the night. It was a difficult evening.

The next morning I decided to go hunting, even though my gear was in bad shape. I walked around for a while, but I didn't see any moose tracks, so I retuned back to camp pretty early. I thought about the broken ski on my Ski-Doo and how I could fix it. I found a tree branch that was twisted at the end, kind of like a ski. I broke it off and then I used my rough axe to carve it into more of a ski shape. Then I tied the wooden ski really tightly to the broken one. When it looked like it would hold, I got on my Ski-Doo and took off for Déline.

In all my years as a hunter, I never experienced as much trouble as I had in that trip to Whiskeyjack Point. It just goes to show that you should always be prepared for the unexpected and ready to do whatever it takes to survive.

Tragedies of the Past

This is a sad story told by Wilson Pelissey's mother, who is Gwich'in from the Fort MacPherson area.

THIS HAPPENED when I was small and travelling in the mountains, way back a long time ago, with my parents.

One time us kids were playing outside by the river, sliding down the riverbank in a toboggan. It was at night and the moonlight was bright, which made it a lot of fun. After we had played for a while, we decided to try sliding down the bank with a full load of kids in the same sled. We all jumped on the sled, some of us sitting and some standing up, and it went down the bank very fast.

We were almost at the bottom of the hill when the toboggan hit something solid and we all flew off. All of us landed on the kid who had been sitting at the very front of the toboggan, and we crushed him. His stomach opened and his intestines were strewn all over the place. He died right there in front of us.

Another time, when we were moving around and living off the land, one of our hunters shot a moose. One of the young men was asked to go pick up the moose with his dog team and bring it back.

When he got to the place where the dead moose was waiting, he began to load it up, but he couldn't ignore how hungry he was. It was such a fat moose with so much extra fat on it that he thought he could eat some without anyone missing it. He started eating that fat while he loaded the rest of the meat, just eating the fat but eating a lot of it.

When he got back to the camp, he was vomiting. He had eaten too much raw moose fat and it was starting to expand in his stomach. It expanded so much that it plugged his airway and he choked to death. He died in front of our eyes.

IT WAS A SUNDAY at the beginning of July 2002. It was a nice Sunday afternoon. I was sitting at home when my dad, Johnny Neyelle, walked in my house after Mass. I grabbed a cup, poured a cup of tea, and set it in front of my dad.

"*Máhci*," he said. I was wondering why he came to my house as he usually did that only if something was important.

He didn't talk much. Then he said, "Follow me. I want to show you something." I put on my jacket and started following my dad, who was walking toward the gravesite. When we got there, we prayed over my brother Ted's grave.

After praying, my dad grabbed a short stick and marked the ground just behind my brother's gravesite. He drew a shape two by six feet— the size of a coffin. He looked at me and said, "I saw this in my dreams. When I die, I want you to bury me here."

I didn't say anything, wondering why he was saying this to me, thinking maybe his time was coming.

Sure enough, two weeks later in the early morning, my sister Grace knocked on my door, saying, "Dad is really sick, we need you to come over right away." I dressed without washing and ran over to my dad's house. I saw my dad sleeping on his bed. He said, "I don't feel good."

I stayed around fifteen minutes or so, then I walked back to my house thinking he should be okay. About five minutes later, my nephew runs in, saying, "My sister Grace wants you over now!"

I walked back to my dad's house and saw my dad still sleeping on his bed. This time he said, "My time has come. I want to shake your hands before I go." My mom, two of my sisters, and my brother shook my dad's hand. Then it was my turn, so I walked up to him and I grabbed his hands. He said, "My son, don't worry too much. You will be okay." Then he said his last word: "Goodbye."

My mind raced back to when I was young, when I would pray wherever I was and ask the Creator to let my dad die in front of me and not while I'm somewhere else. Now that time had come. I watched as my dad breathed his last breath of fresh air and disappeared in front of me forever.

I was fifty-one years old then. I wasn't all there then, my mind was everywhere. I was thinking to myself, "It's not a goodbye, you go where you're going and I'll catch up later because I still have a life to finish here on this earth."

My mom, sisters, and brothers were all crying as I walked out and went home. I was all alone in my bedroom and there I cried for two hours by myself. I remembered a verse in the Good Book that says, "Mourn for at least three days for loved ones and then think about your life again." I also remembered what our Elders were saying about a time like this, how there's a time when you have to start thinking about your own life again. I got up, washed up, and walked over to my mom's house, promising myself that I had done enough crying and I would start thinking about my life now.

There were a lot of relatives from surrounding communities there to visit my dad. I made a coffin for Dad right away, and on the third day it was the funeral service.

Me and four of my brothers walked over to the gravesite and I saw the marking my dad had made and the stick still there where my dad had placed it. I told them this is where my dad showed me a while ago that he wants to be buried when he goes. We started to dig. When we got to about five feet it was time to level it off. I jumped in and held the shovel. I was thinking to my dad, "Now you're gone from the earth. I will be without a dad from now on, but please give me something in return that will tell me that you will always be with me to the end."

I started levelling off the bottom of the grave, which is made of fine sand. Then I struck something solid. I brushed the fine sand with my hands when out came a glittering piece of round stone a couple of inches long. It had a white symbol in the centre of it, but I couldn't figure out what it was. I said, "Dad, *máhci* for the gift!" I felt good after that and accepted my dad's passing.

That day, after the funeral service, we buried my dad, Johnny Neyelle. He lived from 1915 to 2002. Since that day, I always carry my rock wherever I go, knowing he's with me.

Three years after that, close to Christmas, we went to bed late in the evening and a dream came to me. I saw myself going to a gravesite and from a distance I saw my dad's grave. Suddenly, I saw two spirits come out of the grave, which scared me, so I started running back to my house, thinking, "Once I get there I should be safe." But I tripped and fell just before I reached my house. When I looked at the ground, I saw two sets of footprints stopped beside me. I didn't see anybody, so I reached out and my hand bumped against an ankle! That's when I heard my dad saying, "Yes, it's me, my son." I wondered what the other set of footprints was.

Then Dad said, "There's another person here, from a ptarmigan family." Then my dad says to me, "Remember that rock I gave you? Make a case for it and a strap to hang it in your house. If it moves or shakes, a lot of people will fall. And when it falls down, it will be the end of the world."

I opened my eyes and realized it was a dream, a dream about Dad and the rock. I got up. It was four in the morning. I made tea while wondering about the dream. I grabbed the rock and looked at it closely and noticed a small white ptarmigan sitting in the centre of it. I never saw that before, and now it's there...maybe it's telling me something.

I hope God will give me peace and a good life. We will see what the future holds. *Máhci cho*!

Afterword

The Editing Process

IN GENERAL, the versions of the stories that appear in this book came about in the following way. Morris transcribed Johnny's recorded stories into Slavey syllabics or English words, and then he more fully translated them into a literal English rendering. Alana then edited these transcriptions, with input from Morris, into what we call, with some irony, "fixed English."

North Slavey words remain where there is no close equivalent in English, and in these cases an approximate English rendering often follows the Slavey. In many cases we have also chosen to maintain a Slavey word where there is an English cognate, in cases where the place, person, or animal in question are better understood through the Slavey word than its English substitute.

Slavey orthography continues to evolve, and although some of the sounds have standard written forms, others have multiple options or no standard form. We have enlisted the help of orthographer Jane Modeste to produce the spellings we use throughout this collection. We have included a glossary of these North Slavey words.

Editorial decisions about the arrangement and retention of stories were taken collaboratively. For ease of use, and following examples like George Blondin's story collection, *When the World Was New*, the book has been divided into two sections: one for older, distant-time stories and another for more recent life histories. This is not to suggest that these two categories are mutually exclusive or even essentially different; the various stories could easily be told in a different arrangement. Rather, these two sections reflect how the stories were recorded, with distant past and more recent stories told in separate groups.

We have chosen not to include stories in which the majority of plot elements are repeated elsewhere. Instead, we have collated different elements from multiple versions of a given story into a single, more-detailed version. This occurred in three cases: two versions of "The Man Who Lived with a Giant" were blended to provide the version printed in the first section; two short philosophical speeches Johnny made at the beginning of the story recording process—originally titled "Johnny Neyelle Story" and "The Philosophy of Dene People"—have been combined into the introduction from Johnny that prefaces this volume; and one story of Johnny's, titled "My World, My Life," has been left out of the collection due to its close similarities with "Life with My Parents" and "A Trip to Mackenzie Mountain," into which the unique aspects of "My World, My Life" have been integrated.

This approach of combining rather than publishing multiple distinct versions of a given oral text has been criticized in instances where its aim is to produce an "authentic" or correct version of a story, as in the context of salvage ethnography. This is neither the context nor the goal of our approach. By combining stories, we hope only to include all the interesting details Johnny gave to different stories, giving readers a sense of the range and complexity of story elements at play. The stories recorded here are those told by one particular speaker at a particular time in his life. They are not more complete or correct than the versions told by others, but Johnny's skill in storytelling makes them more complex, engaging, and meaningful than others might be.

The stories are illustrated throughout with photos of Johnny at important places in the Northwest Territories, which were graciously provided by Morris Neyelle.

Genealogy of the Extended Neyelle Family

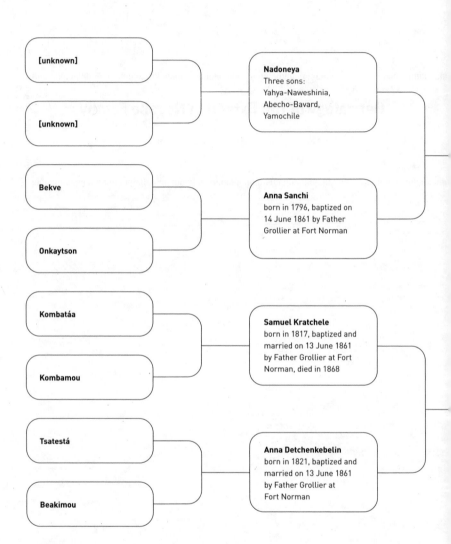

Laurent Yamontchile
born in 1821, baptized on
13 June 1861 by Father
Grollier at Fort Norman,
married on 13 June 1861,
died in 1902 at Wrigley
(Rocky Island)

1. **Madeleine Landle**
2. **Deodat Moses**
3. **Rose Eterika**
4. **Michel Tazo**
5. **Gabriel Tanche**
6. **Jacques Neyally**
7. **Paul Ulla**

Eloiza Etaintse
born in 1835, baptized on
13 June 1861 by Father
Grollier at Fort Norman,
died in 1911 at Wrigley
(Rocky Island)

Father Henri Grollier also
baptized Madeleine Landle
and Deodat Moses in June
1860. Father Grollier died
at Fort Good Hope on 4 June
1864. He was thirty-eight
years old. He is buried at
Good Hope.

This genealogical information was adapted from a list compiled by Father H. Posset at Fort Norman in January 1988, based on Roman Catholic mission records. Updates have been provided by members of the extended Neyelle family.

LAURENT YAMONTCHILE (1821–1902)

- Born in 1821
- Baptized and married on 31 June 1861 by Father Grollier at Fort Norman
- Died in 1902 at Wrigley

and

ELOIZA ETAINTSE (1835–1911)

- Born in 1835
- Died in 1911 at Wrigley

Had a family of seven children:

1. MADELEINE LANDLE
2. DEODAT MOSES
3. ROSE ETERIKA
4. MICHEL TAZO
5. GABRIEL TANCHE
6. JACQUES NEYELLE
7. PAUL ULLA

1. **MADELEINE LANDLE** (1856–?) – Married Charles Betchi on 21 August 1905

- **JULIEN YENDO** (1885–1978) – Married Layza Tazo (1900–1978) on 17 June 1917
  - JOHN YENDO (1925)
  - CECILIA YENDO (1938)
    - *SALLY* (1961)
    - *BRENDA* (1970)
- **MARIE LANDLE** (1897–1980) – Married Jean-Baptiste Antseti (1885–1961) on 17 June 1917
  - ELIZABETH ANTSETI (1916) – Married Albert Horesay (1911) in 1941
    - *VIOLET HORESAY* (1941)
    - *ARCHIE HORESAY* (1942)
    - *DAVID HORESAY* (1944)
    - *ALFRED HORESAY* (1951)
    - *ROSE MARY HORESAY* (1952)
    - *LUCY HORESAY* (1954)
    - *MERILEE HORESAY* (MacCauley) (1960)
    - *JESSIE HORESAY*
  - ADELE ANTSETI (1925) – Married George Hardisty (1919) in 1947
    - *GABRIEL HARDISTY* (1945) and Elsie Ekenale (1947)
      - Gloria (1973)
      - Ettona (1977)
      - Nicole (1980)
    - *HENRY HARDISTY* (1948)
    - *ETHEL HARDISTY* (1949) and Philip Liske
    - *JANE HARDISTY* (1953)
    - *VIOLET HARDISTY* (1960)
    - *SHIRLEY HARDISTY* (1961)
    - *WALTER HARDISTY* (1964)

- CHRISTINE ANTSETI (1927) – Married Sonny Arthur Hardisty (1923) in 1939
  - *CHARLES HARDISTY* (1946)
  - *EDWARD JAMES HARDISTY* (1949)
  - *SAMUEL PERCY HARDISTY* (1951)
- MARY ANTSETI (1927) – Married Edward Neyally (1921) in 1957

2. DEODAT MOSES (1860–1946) – Married Marie Tseante in 1904
- **PHILIP MOSES (NEKENEYA)** (1889–1986) – Married Marie-Louise Yendi (1903) in 1920
  - JAMES MOSES (1922) – Married Lena Peter (1954)
    - *WENDY* (1977)
    - *JAMES JR.* (1980)
  - CAROLINE MOSES (1927) – Married Wilson Pelissey (1910) in 1947
    - *ALICE* (1947)
    - *SARAH* (1951)
    - *MARY* (1952)
    - *LENA* (1955)
    - *MICHAEL* (1956)
    - *BERNICE* (1958)
    - *DORIS* (1960)
    - *DIANE* (1962)
    - *CATHY* (1964)
    - *SHARON* (1965)
    - *FREDA* (1966)
    - *RAYMOND* (1968)
  - MARGUERITE MOSES (1930) and Edward Hardisty (1917)
    - *ALBERT MOSES* (1951)
    - *DAVID* (1958)
    - *GEORGE MOSES* (1959)
    - *ERNIE MOSES* (1961)

- *LLOYD MOSES* (1963)
- *JERRY MOSES* (1965)
- *ROSE-MARY MOSES* (1966)
- *BETTY-ANN MOSES* (1968)
- *DARCY MOSES* (1970)
- *MORRIS MOSES* (1972)
- CORRINE MOSES (1934)
- ROSA MOSES (1935)
  - *STEVE MOSES* (1956)
  - *FLOYD MOSES* (1961)
- LEON MOSES (1938)
- DENISE MOSES (1940)
- LAURA MOSES (1945)
- **PAUL (MOSES) EKENALE** (1911) – Married Helen Betsedea (1925)
  - ANGUS EKENALE (1945) – Married Rosa Denerou
    - 3 children
  - ELSIE EKENALE (1947) – Married Gabriel Hardisty (1945) in 1972
    - *GLORIA HARDISTY* (1973)
    - *ETONA HARDISTY* (1977)
    - *NICOLE* (1980)
  - ALMA EKENALE (1949)
  - LUCIE EKENALE (1952)
  - RUFUS EKENALE (1952)
  - RICHARD EKENALE (1954)
  - RUBY EKENALE (1958)
  - JONAS EKENALE (1960)
  - DANIEL EKENALE (1966)
  - RICKY EKENALE (1971)
- **MARGUERITE MOSES** (1913) – Married Frank Horesay (1909) in 1934
  - JOHN HORESAY (1935–1974)
  - ROSY HORESAY (1937)
  - FLORENCE HORESAY (1939) – Married Alfred Antoine (1935–1977)

- *WILFRED ANTOINE* (1962)

- *URBAN ANTOINE* (1964)

- *GILBERT ANTOINE* (1965)

- *DIANE ANTOINE* (1966)

- *WALLY ANTOINE* (1967)

- Remarried in 1982 to Charles Hardisty (1946)

  - *CAWLLEY HARDISTY* (1981)

- CELINE HORESAY (1941) – Married George Campbell (1937) in 1961

  - *FABIEN CAMPBELL* (1961)

  - *CLARENCE CAMPBELL* (1964)

  - *FLOYD CAMPBELL* (1965)

  - *BERTON CAMPBELL* (1966)

  - *LAWRENCE CAMPBELL* (1973)

  - *GLORY-ANN CAMPBELL* (1979)

- DAVID HORESAY (1942)

- JANE HORESAY (1944–1980)

- ARCHIE HORESAY (1946)

- CHRISTINE HORESAY (1948)

- MARY-ALICE HORESAY (1950) – Married Lucas Cli (1941–1977) in 1970

  - *TAMMY CLI* (1971)

  - *TRINA CLI* (1973)

  - *TANIS CLI* (1974)

  - *TIU CLI* (1977)

- MABEL HORESAY (1954)

- SARAH HORESAY (1955)

- WILFRED HORESAY (1965)

- RIA HORESAY (1972)

3. ROSE ETERIKA – Married Paul Za (died in 1902)

- No children

4. **MICHEL TAZO** (died in 1905) – Married Marguerite Membe

- **LAYZA TAZO** (1900-1978) – Married Julien Yendo (1885-1978) on 17 June 1917

5. **GABRIEL TANCHE** (1870-1950) – Married Rosalie Membette (1880-??) on 18 June 1902

- **FRANCIS TANCHE** (1901-1973) – Married Marie Etata (1910-1946) on 26 June 1927

  - JOHNNY TANCHE (1929) – Married Denise Bouvier (1936) in 1959

    - *ROBERT TANCHE* (1962)
    - *DARYL TANCHE* (1964)
    - *DEBORAH TANCHE* (1965)

  - WILLIAM TANCHE (1930) – Married Marie-Jane Michel (1942) in 1962

    - *MORRIS TANCHE* (1959)
    - *SANDRA TANCHE* (1961)
    - *CATHERINE TANCHE* (1962)
    - *MARY TANCHE* (1964)
    - *DENNIS TANCHE* (1965)
    - *LINDA TANCHE* (1967)
    - *RAYMOND TANCHE* (1968)
    - *BEVERLY TANCHE* (1969)
    - *DANIEL TANCHE* (1971)
    - *JERRY TANCHE* – deceased

  - ALICE TANCHE (1936) and Joe Villeneuve

    - *MILDRED TANCHE* (1961)
    - *STEPHEN TANCHE* (1963) – deceased
    - *JOSEPH TANCHE* (1964)
    - *BRENDA TANCHE* (1966)
    - *BETTY TANCHE* (1968)
    - *JOS.-JOHN TANCHE* (1970) – deceased

6. JACQUES NEYELLE (1877-1953) - Married Marie Kotoyeneh (1880-1946) on 21 August 1905 (daughter of Enaye and Bekoro)

- **ALBERT NEYELLE** (1905-1972) - Married Marguerite Bavard (1913-1931) on 26 June 1927
  - LEON NEYELLE (1929)
- Remarried on 27 July 1933 to Elizabeth Pelissey
  - JONAS NEYELLE (1945) - Married Rose Bavard (1937) in 1965
    - *RONALD NEYELLE* (1968, adopted)
  - ROSE RUTH NEYELLE-YENDO (1952-1969)
- **CHARLES MARIE NEYELLE** (1906-??)
- **MARY NEYELLE** (1909-1914)
- **BONIFACE NEYELLE** (1910) - Married widow Dorah Yendi (1922) in 1956
  - ROSE-MARY NEYELLE (1959-1960)
  - MARY JANE NAYALLY (1962) - Married Gilbert Cazon
    - *BIANCA* (1982)
    - *SHANNON CAZON* (1988)
    - *DYLAN CAZON* (1993)
    - *CHANTEL CAZON* (1994)
- **GEORGE NAYALLY** (1913-1955) - Married Dorah Yendi (1922) on 7 September 1942
  - CELINA NAYALLY (1943-1943)
  - JOHNNY NAYALLY (1944-1944)
  - CHRISTINE NAYALLY (1945-1949)
  - ANNY NAYALLY (1947-1948)
  - FREDERICK NAYALLY (1949-1984) - Married Mary Jane Betseda on 25 October 1981
    - *MICHELLE ROSE NAYALLY* (1976)
    - *ARSENE NAYALLY* (1980)
    - *LAWRENCE NAYALLY* (1984)
    - *JEFFREY NAYALLY*
  - ERNESTINE NAYALLY (1951-1952)
  - DARCY NAYALLY (1953-1953)

- SARAH NAYALLY (1954) and Timmy Lennie (1956)
  - *ETANDA* (1982)
  - *FREDDY* (1986)
- **JOHNNY NEYELLE** (1915–2002) – Married Rose-Marie Simon
  - CHARLES NEYELLE (1944) – Married Georgina Menacho (1953) in 1970
    - *FRIEDA NEYELLE* (1970)
    - *SIMON NEYELLE* (1972)
    - *IVENESSA NEYELLE*
- Remarried in 1950 to Jane Kenny (1933)
  - MAURICE [MORRIS] NEYELLE (1951) – Married Bernice Taniton (1956) in 1975
    - *GLORIA NEYELLE* (1975)
    - *LYLE NEYELLE* (1978)
    - *ISRAEL NEYELLE* (1982)
  - MICHAEL NEYELLE (1956) – Married Julia Bonnetplume
  - TED NEYELLE (1962–1990) – Married Suzan Mackeinzo (1960) in 1982
    - *JOYCE NEYELLE* (1982)
    - *KEITH NEYELLE* (1983)
    - *LORRAINE NEYELLE* (1984)
    - *ANTHONY NEYELLE* (1985)
    - *SHEENA NEYELLE* (1987)
  - GRACE NEYELLE (1963)
    - *MORAN-LEE NEYELLE* (1982)
    - *KAYLA NEYELLE* (1987)
  - PAULINA TETSO (1965, adopted) – Married Kevin Roache
    - *CARSON ROACHE*
    - *JAKE ROACHE*
    - *DALLAS ROACHE*
    - *JOHNNY ROACHE*
  - THOMAS NEYELLE (1967) – Common-law Celine Mantla
    - *MORGAN NEYELLE* (1968)

- KENNY NEYELLE (1968) – Common-law Beatrace Whane
  - *TRAYLINE*
  - *KENDRA*
- **PAUL NEYELLE** (1919–2004)
- **EDWARD NEYELLE** (1921–??) – Married Mary Antseti-Neyelle (1934) in 1957
  - LAUREEN NAYALLY (1958)
  - MARTHA NAYALLY (1959) and Michael Drake
    - *MATTHEW DRAKE* (1985–1997)
    - *MELANIE DRAKE*
    - *[unknown]*
  - GRACE NAYALLY (1960) and David Williams
  - PHOEBE NAYALLY (1962) and Richard Ekenale (1954)
    - *SASHA* (1982)
    - *[unknown]*
  - JOSEPH NAYALLY (1963)
  - KEITH NAYALLY (1964) and Helen Vital
  - ROBERT NAYALLY (1966) and Sally Yendo
  - GILBERT NEYELLE (1969)
  - MICHAEL NEYELLE JR. (1970–2015)
    - *JOSHUA LAFFERTY*

7. **PAUL ULLA** (1881–1931) – Married Elise Etata
   - No children

bebaa: Nephew, niece

bechile: Younger brother

bedzikat'į: Chief hunter

bega: A white stone

Begáhdé: Keele River

Begáyué: Mountain range

béhdzįga: Snowy owl

betá: Father

betsée: Grandfather; also grandson, grandchild

betsį: Grandmother

daht'o: A stage; a platform

Dehcho: Mackenzie River

Déline: Where the waters flow (Fort Franklin)

denek'á: Throat

Dewadé: Celine River

dih: Spruce grouse

ele: Bough

Ɂemǫǫhdzí: Cougar; also Lion people

éne: Mother

eseh-gokwi: A place in the Mackenzie Mountains

Ets'ıhch'e: Period of transformation from boyhood to manhood

e-tseh-toh: A place in the Mackenzie Mountains

ʔEyǫnę náréhya: The standings of Ayonia's warriors

gokw'i ejiré: Muskox

gólerécho: A big drywood area

ık'ǫ: Medicine power

ık'ǫzhiné: Medicine song

itá: (My) father

K'áhbamñtúé: Ptarmigan net place (Colville Lake)

K'áshogot'ine: Hare people

k'áté: Willow Flats

kǫtú erıhtlı: The Book of Alcohol

Kwechádé: A river

Kwenáréhya: Where the rocks are standing

Kwetenıa: A lake

máhci: Thank you

náhʔácho: Dinosaurs

Nahʔane: Yukon people

Náts'ıhch'o: A mountain ridge

Néréla: Sets across

ni-cha: A river

nǫgha: Wolverine

qua-da-lee: A river

Rádeyîlîkóé: Rapids place (Fort Good Hope)

sahcho: Grizzly bear

Sahtúot'ine: Bear Lake people

senǫ: (My) mother, (my) auntie

Shúhtaot'ine: Mountain people

Taʔąle: Fish Lake

Tǎegōhtî: Where there is oil (Norman Wells)

tah-ga-ra-lee: A river

teh-oh-cho-wah: A place in the Mackenzie Mountains where people
   gather for caribou migration in the fall

tehk'áe: Muskrat

Tets'chxe: Drum Lake

Tłdedele daetł'ı: Tied Red-dog Ridge

tł'o k'áe: Willow grass

Tłok'á nái?a: Grass standing up

to-ka-toeh: Blackwater Lake

Tugǫtúé: Keller Lake

Tuts'ınılı: Flows toward the lake

Tútsituwé: Loon Lake

tse-tsee: A place where there are flats

ts'u: Spruce

Tulita: Where the waters meet (Fort Norman)

weh-zia: A river

xáhtǫnę: Strangers

Yíhda: The Big Dipper

Other Titles from University of Alberta Press

People of the Lakes

Stories of Our Van Tat Gwich'in Elders/
Googwandak Nakhwach'ànjòo Van Tat Gwich'in
VUNTUT GWITCHIN FIRST NATION &
SHIRLEEN SMITH
Fifty years of Elders' oral histories recount 150
years of Gwich'in life in Canada's North.

Wisdom Engaged

Traditional Knowledge for Northern
Community Well-being
LESLIE MAIN JOHNSON, *Editor*
Collaboration between traditional knowledge
and Western bio-medicine aims to improve
health care in Northern communities.
Patterns of Northern Traditional Healing Series

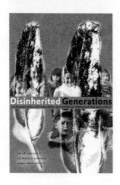

Disinherited Generations

Our Struggle to Reclaim Treaty Rights for
First Nations Women and their Descendants
NELLIE CARLSON & KATHLEEN
STEINHAUER *with* LINDA GOYETTE
Two Cree women fought injustices regarding
the rights of Indigenous women and children
in Canada.

More information at uap.ualberta.ca